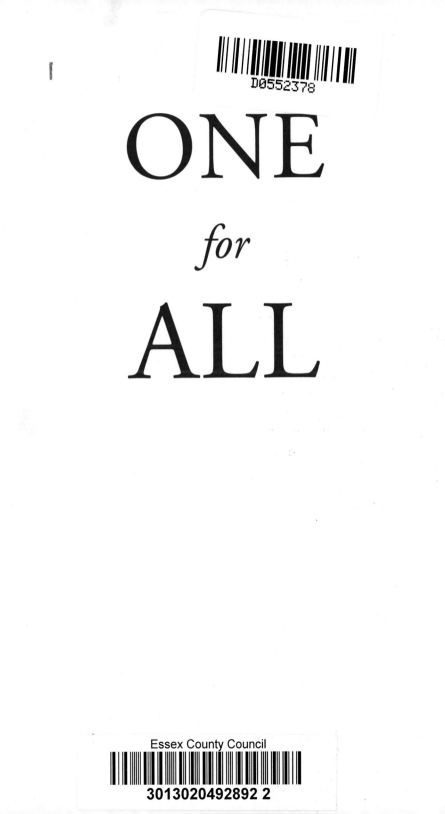

ONE

for

ALL

ONE

for

ALL

*From four well known reports comes
one account of one man who changed
the world*

Compiled and Arranged by

JOHN SWIFT

Matador
9 Priory Business Park,
Wistow Road, Kibworth Beauchamp,
Leicestershire. LE8 0RX
Tel: (+44) 116 279 2299
Fax: (+44) 116 279 2277
Email: books@troubador.co.uk
Web: www.troubador.co.uk/matador

ISBN 978 1780884 462

British Library Cataloguing in Publication Data.
A catalogue record for this book is available from the British Library.

Printed and bound in the UK by TJ International, Padstow, Cornwall
Typeset in 11pt Aldine401 BT Roman by Troubador Publishing Ltd, Leicester, UK

Matador is an imprint of Troubador Publishing Ltd

Dedications

This book is dedicated first to those who wouldn't want to be seen reading a Bible but who would like to know what the story of Jesus is all about, and secondly to all those who over the last 2000 years have helped to put the Bible into languages that people can understand – sometimes at the cost of their own lives.

Thanks

Thanks to all those who have encouraged me in this work by asking after its progress, in particular Lionel Currie. Thanks too to my proof-readers – John Braine and my brother David – and others for their helpful and critical comments. And last but not least to Joy for her support and putting up with my frequent trips to the study and numerous bookshops.

Contents

Preface

Over 50% of the population of the United Kingdom identify themselves as 'Christian'. However, it is clear from quiz shows, general conversations and aspects of national life that, today, most people know very little of the Bible, not even the short gospel narratives – the stories of Jesus – which are the basis of the Christian faith. Perhaps a reason for this lack of knowledge could be that the four gospels are often set in small print and columns amongst the rest of the 66 books of the seemingly formidable library we know as 'the Bible'.

In order to make the gospels more readily accessible to today's byte-size world, the following pages provide one integrated story of the 'good news' as told by Matthew, Mark, Luke and John. So the more familiar chapters and verses of the four gospels may not be easily identified in this work.

An additional explanation about my use of some words can be found in the pages at the end of the main text. End Notes provide background information on some aspects of Judaism.

The text has been drawn from several Bible translations and the views of some commentators which have not found their way into any translation. I am responsible for the chapter headings and sub-headings, the sequencing of the script and the occasional paraphrasing.

In preparing this material I have been struck by the uniqueness and authenticity of the gospel message. It rings true. It does not come across as the product of someone's fertile imagination; indeed there are numerous indications that these really are eye-witness accounts. The overall message is that God has invaded planet earth to set up a kingdom altogether different from the empires of men and that he is reaching out to the human race, with whom He longs to have a relationship. It is evident throughout that God hates religion and ritual that hinder people from knowing Him. This explains the almost incessant antagonism of the religious leaders to the message and person of Jesus.

My hope is that in reading this book you will discover the 'darling of heaven' and perhaps gain a fresh understanding of what the four 'Bible' gospels are saying. You may then want to go back and read the individual gospels themselves. Above all, as John says at the end of his gospel, I trust that you will come 'to believe in his name' for yourself.

JDS, Leeds, April 2011

PART 1

The Early Days
&
The Coming of the King

CHAPTER 1

Preparing the Way

Foreword

Dearest Loved by God,

It is well known that many people have already compiled a written account of the remarkable, prophecy-fulfilling, events that happened among us. The information was handed down by those who were eye-witnesses and who became servants and proclaimers of the message. Since I too have investigated the facts in the minutest detail, from the very beginning, it seemed right for me also to write an orderly narrative for you. So that you may know with certainty the truth about the stories you have been taught.

A brief summary of the whole story, time and eternity!

Before time began there was *The Supreme Being*[1] who was with God, and in fact was God. All things came into being through him; indeed without him nothing came into existence. In him was LIFE, and this LIFE brought light to humanity. The light is still shining in the darkness, and the darkness has never ever, and will never, ever put it out.

There appeared in history a man sent from God; his name was John. He came as a witness to tell people about that light, so that everyone might believe. John himself was not the light; he simply came as a witness to the light. The True Light which enlightens everyone was coming into the world.

He – the True Light – entered the world, yet even though the whole cosmos was made through him, the people of the world did not recognise him. He came to the domain prepared for him, but his own people did not accept him. Yet to all those who did receive him, to those who believed what he said and put their trust in him, he gave the privilege and the power to become children of God – children born not by human descent, desire nor decision, but born by God.

So The Supreme Being became a human being and pitched in among us. We saw his glorious splendour – close up; the glorious splendour of the Treasured One who came from the Father; he was full of grace and truth. Out of his unlimited supply we all continue to receive one undeserved blessing after another. You see, God's law was mediated through Moses; but grace and the truth are communicated through the *Christ*[2] – Jesus. No-one has ever seen God, except God the One and Only Darling, who is intimately one with the Father, he has made him known.

Inconceivable conceptions

The good news about Jesus, the Christ, the Son of God, started like this:

During the time when Herod (The Great) was king of Judea, there was a certain priest named Zechariah, who belonged to the priestly order of Abijah; his wife Elizabeth was also a direct descendant of Aaron. Both of them lived upright lives in the sight of God, fully and blamelessly observing all the Lord's commandments and regulations. But they had no children, because Elizabeth was infertile; now they were both well advanced in years.

It happened that it was the turn of Zechariah's order to be on duty, to serve in the temple (in Jerusalem) close to where the presence of God was. According to the custom of the priesthood, by lot, Zechariah was chosen to enter the temple and burn incense. During the time when the incense was being burnt, and the crowd of assembled worshippers was praying outside, one of the Lord's angels appeared, standing at the right side of the incense-altar. When Zechariah saw him, he was terrified and paralysed with fear. But the angel said to him, "Don't be afraid, Zechariah; your prayer – the one you used to pray – has been heard. Your wife Elizabeth will bear you a son; you must give him the name 'John'. He will not only be your pride and joy, but many people will rejoice at his birth. He must not drink wine nor spirits because he will be great in the sight of the Lord, being filled with the Holy Spirit while still in his mother's womb. He will turn many of the people of Israel back to the Lord their God. He will go as the Lord's herald, in the spirit and power of Elijah, to turn the hearts of fathers towards their children. He will cause the disobedient to repent of their sins and turn to the wise ways of the Lord – to make people perfectly prepared for the Lord."

Zechariah asked the angel, "How can I possibly believe this? I'm an old man and my wife is past the age of child-bearing."

"I am Gabriel", the angel answered. "I stand in the very presence of God. He sent me to talk to you and to bring you this good news. But now, because you didn't believe my words, which will come true at the proper time, you'll lose your power of speech and remain silent until the day this happens."

Meanwhile, the people were waiting for Zechariah, wondering why he lingered so long in the temple. When finally he came out, he could not speak to them and because he tried to explain himself by making signs to them, yet remaining speechless, they realised he had seen a vision in the temple.

When Zechariah had completed his time of service, he went back home. Afterwards his wife Elizabeth became pregnant. She remained in seclusion for five months saying, "The Lord himself has done this for me. In these days he has looked with favour on me and taken away the shame I've felt when I was among my people."

In the sixth month of Elizabeth's pregnancy God sent Gabriel to a town in Galilee called Nazareth, to a virgin named *Mary*[3] who was engaged to a man named Joseph. Approaching her, the angel said, "Rejoice most favoured one! The Lord is with you."

Mary was greatly perplexed at his words and wondered what this greeting might mean. But Gabriel said to her, "Don't be afraid, Mary. God is well-pleased with you. Listen: you're going to become pregnant and give birth to a son. You'll name him *Jesus*. He will be a great man and will be called the Son of the Most High. The Lord God will give him the throne of his forefather, David. He will reign over the house of Jacob for ever; and his kingdom will never end."

"How can this be," Mary asked, "since I'm a virgin?"

Gabriel answered, "The Holy Spirit will come to you, the power of the Most High will overshadow you. So the child to be born will be holy; he will be called the Son of God. Even Elizabeth your relative, she too has conceived a son in her old age, so the one whom they called 'Barren' is six months pregnant. For no word of God is impossible to fulfil."

"Here I am, the Lord's servant", Mary responded. "Let it happen to me just as you've said." Then the angel left her.

A magnificent muse

Then and there, Mary got ready and hurried off to a village in the hill country of Judea, where she entered Zechariah's house and greeted Elizabeth. When Elizabeth heard Mary's greeting, the baby leaped in her womb, and Elizabeth was filled with the Holy Spirit. With a loud cry she exclaimed: "Blessed are you among women, and blessed is the fruit of your womb! But why have I this privilege that the mother of my Lord should come to visit me? See, as soon as I heard the sound of your greeting, the baby in my womb leaped for joy. How blessed is she who has believed that there will be a fulfilment of what was told her from the Lord!"

Then Mary burst out singing: "My soul proclaims the greatness of the Lord, my spirit rejoices in God my Saviour, because he noticed the lowly status of this maiden. From now on all generations will call me blessed, for the Mighty One has done great things for me; Holy is his name.

His mercy embraces those who fear him, from generation to generation.

He performs mighty deeds with his arm;

He scatters the haughty;

He deposes dynasties from their thrones, but lifts up the humble.

He fills the hungry with good things, but sends the rich away – empty.

In mercy he has reached out his hand to Israel, his servant; forever remembering what he spoke to our forefathers, to Abraham and his offspring."

Mary remained with Elizabeth for about three months, and then returned to her own home.

Name and fame

When Elizabeth's full term came, she gave birth to a son. Her neighbours and relatives heard that the Lord had multiplied his great mercy towards her, so they rejoiced with her. On the eighth day they came to circumcise the baby and were going to name him Zechariah, after his father. But his mother intervened saying, "No! No! He's to be called John."

They said to her, "None of your relatives has that name." So they began making signs to his father, to find out what he wanted the child to be called. He asked for a little writing tablet, and to everyone's amazement he wrote, 'His name is John'. Immediately Zechariah's mouth opened, his tongue was loosed and he began speaking and praising God.

Then Zechariah was filled with the Holy Spirit and prophesied: "Praise be to the Lord, the God of Israel, because he's visited and redeemed his people.

He has raised up a strong saviour for us in the house of David, his servant.

It's just as he promised through his holy prophets from the beginning of time:

to save us from our enemies and from the hand of all who hate us –

to show us mercy, and

to remember his holy covenant – the oath he swore to our forefather Abraham, whereby we would be able us to serve him without fear, in his presence; living in holiness and righteousness all our days.

As for you, my child, you will be called the prophet of the Most High. You'll go on ahead of the Lord to prepare his way:

to give to his people knowledge of salvation by the forgiveness of their sins;

to reveal the compassionate heart of our God, by which a new dawn will break upon us;

to give light to those living in darkness and in the shadow of death, and

to guide our feet into the way of peace."

The fear of God filled the neighbourhood, and throughout all the hill country of Judea people were thinking and talking about these things, asking, "What's going to become of this child?" as it was evident that the Lord's hand was on him.

The child grew and became strong in spirit. (He lived in the wilderness until the day he appeared publicly to Israel.)

A stable background

This is how the birth of Jesus, the Christ, came about:

Before she had sexual relations with Joseph, Mary was found to be pregnant. Because Joseph, her husband-to-be, was an upright man, and did not want to make her notorious by exposing her to public disgrace, he planned to annul their engagement secretly.

But just as he considered this, the angel from the Lord appeared to him in a dream saying, "Joseph, son of David, don't be afraid to take Mary as your wife, because what is conceived in her is from the Holy Spirit. She will give birth to a son, and you are to give him the name Jesus, because he is the one who will save his people from their sins."

[All this took place to fulfil what the Lord had said through the prophet: "Look! The virgin will be pregnant and will give birth to a son, and they will call his name 'Immanuel' (which means, 'God is with us')."]

When Joseph woke from sleep, he did what the angel had commanded him: he took Mary as his wife, but he had no sexual union with her until after she gave birth to a son.

A short while later Caesar Augustus issued a decree that the population of the entire empire should be registered. (This was the census which took place before the one taken while Quirinius was governor of Syria.) Everyone had to travel to their own town of origin to be registered. So Joseph went with Mary, from Nazareth to Judea, to the town of David called Bethlehem, because he was a descendant of David.

While they were there, the time came for the baby to be born. Mary gave birth to her firstborn – a son. She wrapped him snugly in strips of cloths and laid him in a feeding trough, because there was no space for them in the guest-room.

Shepherds see a lamb[4]

In the same area there were shepherds camping out in the fields, keeping guard over their flocks during the night. Suddenly one of the Lord's angels appeared at their side, and the brilliant splendour of the Lord shone around them. They were terrified. But the angel said to them, "Don't be afraid. Look, I'm announcing to you good news of great joy that will be for all people. Today, in the town of David, a Saviour has been born – he is the Messiah, the Lord. This is how you'll know him: you'll find a baby lying in a feeding trough, snugly wrapped in strips of cloth."

Then suddenly, there appeared with the angel a great company of heaven's angelic army, praising God saying, "Glory to God in the highest. Let there be peace among the peoples of the earth, in whom he delights."

When the angels had returned to heaven, the shepherds said to one another, "Let's go to Bethlehem and see this thing that's happened, which the Lord has told us about."

So they hurried off and found Mary and Joseph, and the baby who was lying in the feeding trough. Having seen them, the shepherds spread the word about what had been told them concerning this child. Everyone was astonished at what was described to them. The shepherds returned to the fields, glorifying and praising God for everything they had heard and seen; which was exactly as they had been told.

Mary treasured all these things; pondering over them in her heart.

Religious observance

On the eighth day, when it was time to circumcise the baby, he was named Jesus, the name the angel had given him before he had been conceived.

After the time for purification according to the Law of Moses, (*a further thirty-three days*), Joseph and Mary took Jesus to Jerusalem to present him to the Lord, and to offer a sacrifice in accordance with the Law of the Lord, which states: '*Every firstborn male opening the womb is to be consecrated to the Lord… with a pair of turtle doves or two young pigeons.*'

There was a man in Jerusalem called Simeon, who was upright and devout. He was waiting for the one who would comfort and encourage Israel. The Holy Spirit had revealed to him that he would not die until he had seen the Lord's Anointed King. Led by the Spirit, he went into the temple. When the parents brought in the child Jesus, Simeon took the baby in his arms and praised God, saying:

"Lord, according to your word, your servant can now die in peace. My eyes have seen your salvation, which you've made available to all peoples – a light of revelation for the nations and glory for your people Israel."

The child's father and mother were astonished at what was being said about him. Then Simeon blessed them and said to Mary, "Take note, this child is destined to cause the rise and fall of many in Israel, and to be a standard that will be opposed, as the thoughts of many hearts will be revealed. Yes, and a sword will pierce your own soul too."

A prophetess, Anna, the daughter of Phanuel, from the tribe of Asher was there that day also. She was eighty-four years old; having lived with her husband for seven years after her marriage, and then was widowed. She never left the temple but worshipped night and day with fastings and prayers. At that same time she approached them and gave thanks to God. Afterwards Anna spoke, to all who were looking forward to the deliverance of Jerusalem, about the child.

When Joseph and Mary had done everything required by the Law, they returned to Bethlehem.

Wise men seek a king

After Jesus was born, *Magians*[5] from the East arrived unexpectedly in Jerusalem and asked, "Where is the one who has been born King of the Judeans? We observed his star in the East and have come to worship him."

When King Herod heard this he became very excited, along with everyone else in Jerusalem. He assembled all the chief priests and the teachers of the people and asked them exactly where the Messiah would be born. "In Bethlehem in Judea," they told him, " because this is what the prophet has written:

'And you, Bethlehem, in the land of Judah,
> are by no means least among the rulers of Judah;
>> for out of you will come a ruler who will
>>> shepherd my people Israel'."

So Herod summoned the Magians secretly. He found out from them the exact time when the star had first appeared. He sent them to Bethlehem saying, "Go and search carefully for the little child. As soon as you find him, report back to me, so that I too may go and worship him."

After they had listened to the king, they departed. And there it was – the star that they had seen in the East. When they saw the star, they were over the moon! It went ahead of them until it stood over the place where the little child was. On entering the house, they saw the child with Mary, and they bowed down and worshipped him. Then they opened their treasure chests and offered him gifts of gold, frankincense and myrrh. But having been warned in a dream not to return to Herod, they travelled back to their own country another way.

Out of Africa

No sooner had they gone, an angel appeared to Joseph in a dream and said, "Wake up, take the young child and his mother, and escape to Egypt. Stay there until I tell you, because Herod is determined to search for the child to destroy him." So Joseph got up during the night, took the child and his mother and left for Egypt. He stayed there until the death of Herod, so fulfilling what the Lord had said through the prophet: 'Out of Egypt I have called my son.'

When Herod realised that he had been outwitted by the Magians, he was furious. He gave orders to kill all the boys who were two years old or younger, in Bethlehem and its surrounding districts, in accordance with the time of birth he had ascertained from the Magians.

[This fulfilled what was said through the prophet Jeremiah:
'A voice was heard in Ramah, weeping and great mourning, Rachel weeping for her children and she would not be comforted, because they are no more.']

After Herod died, an angel appeared again to Joseph in a dream and said, "Rise, take the child and his mother and go to the land of Israel, because those who sought to take the child's life are dead." So he got up, took the child and his mother, and went to the land of Israel. But when he heard that Archelaus was ruling in Judea in place of his father Herod, Joseph was afraid to go back there. Being warned in a dream, he went to the district of Galilee, and returned to live in Nazareth.

[So what was said through the prophets was fulfilled: "He will be called a *Branch*[6]."]

The child continued to grow in stature and strength, and the grace of God was on him.

A Jerusalem journey

Every year Jesus' parents travelled to Jerusalem for the Feast of the Passover. According to the custom, when he was twelve years old,

Jesus went with them to the Feast. After the festival days were over, while his parents were returning home, the boy, Jesus, remained in Jerusalem. But his parents didn't know this; they supposed he was in the caravan. They travelled on for a day, before they began searching for him among their relatives and friends. When they did not find him, they returned to Jerusalem to look for him. After three days they found him in the temple, sitting among the teachers, listening to them and asking them questions. All who heard him were amazed at his intelligence and his answers. When his parents saw him, they too were astonished. His mother said to him, "Son, why did you do this to us? Your father and I have been worried sick, looking all over for you."

"Why were you looking for me?" he asked. "Didn't you know I would now have to start getting involved with my Father's work?" But they did not understand what he was saying.

He returned with them to Nazareth and was obedient to them. His mother treasured all his sayings in her heart.

Jesus kept increasing in wisdom, in stature and in favour with God and men.

MAP OF ISRAEL IN NEW TESTAMENT TIMES

Source: http://www.bible-history.com/maps/palestine_nt_times.html

CHAPTER 2

First Steps

Great Expectations

In the fifteenth year of the reign of the Emperor Tiberius, Pontius Pilate was governor of Judea, Herod Antipas was tetrarch of Galilee, his brother Philip was tetrarch of the region of Iturea and Traconitis, Lysanias was tetrarch of Abilene and Annas with Caiapas were the High Priests. At that time God spoke to John, the son of Zechariah, while he was living in the wilderness. As a result he went into the Judean desert and all the countryside around the river Jordan, preaching and practising a baptism of repentance for the forgiveness of sins saying, "Change your mind and heart, because the kingdom of heaven is coming."

[John was the one written about in the book of Isaiah the prophet:
'See, I will send my messenger before your face, he will prepare your way.
The voice of one calling in the desert, "Prepare the way for the Lord, make his paths straight. Every valley shall be filled in and every mountain and hill made low. The crooked roads shall become straight, the rough paths made smooth roads. And all mankind will see God's salvation."']

John wore clothing made of coarse camel's hair, with a leather belt around his waist. For food he ate locusts and wild honey. Crowds of people, from the whole Judean countryside, the area around the Jordan and all of Jerusalem, flocked to him. On confessing their sins, they were immersed by him in the river Jordan near Bethany (the one on the east side of the river).

When he saw many of the *Pharisees*[7] and *Sadducees*[8] coming to where he was baptising, he said to them: "You brood of vipers! Who warned you to escape from the coming judgement? Produce worthwhile evidence of your repentance and don't presume to say to yourselves, 'We're O.K. We have Abraham as our ancestor.' I tell you that out of these stones God is able to raise up children for Abraham. Already the axe is poised at the root of the trees, and every tree that doesn't produce good fruit will be cut down and thrown into the fire."

"What should we do then?" the crowds asked.

John answered, "Whoever has two shirts should share with him who has none, and whoever has plenty of food should do the same."

Tax collectors also came to be baptised and they asked, "Teacher, what should we do?"

"Don't collect any more than has been set," he told them.

Serving soldiers were also asking him, "So what about us, what should we do?"

He said to them, "Don't extort money from anyone, don't accuse people falsely and be content with your wages."

With expectation rising, the people were all wondering whether John might possibly be The Messiah. Religious leaders from Jerusalem sent a deputation of priests and Levites to ask him who he was. But John consistently and repeatedly stated, "I'm not the Messiah."

They asked him, "Then who are you? Are you Elijah?" "No I'm not," he replied. "Are you The Prophet?" they asked. Again he answered, "No."

Finally they said, "Who are you then? Give us an answer to take back to those who sent us. What do you say about yourself?"

John replied in the words of Isaiah, "I'm 'the voice of someone calling out in the desert, 'Make the road straight for the Lord'."

Some Pharisees, who had been sent, also questioned him, "Why then do you baptise if you're not the Messiah, nor Elijah, nor the Prophet?"

John answered all of them by saying, "I baptise you with water for repentance. But amongst you stands one whom you don't know. He is coming after me and is much mightier than I am. I'm not worthy to carry his sandals nor even bend down and unfasten them. He'll baptise you with the Holy Spirit and fire. His winnowing-fork is in his hand; he'll clear his threshing floor and gather the wheat into his storehouse, but he'll burn up the chaff with unquenchable fire."

With many other words John exhorted the people and preached the good news to them.

The descending dove

Now it happened that when all the people were being baptised, Jesus came from Nazareth in Galilee to the Jordan to be baptised by John too. John saw Jesus coming towards him and declared, "Look, the Lamb of God, who takes away the sinfulness of the world! This is the one I spoke about when I said, 'A man comes after me who outranks me because he existed before me'. I myself didn't recognise him, but the reason I came baptising with water was that he might be revealed to Israel."

John tried to prevent Jesus from being baptised, saying, "I need to be baptised by you, yet you come to me?"

But Jesus replied, "Let it be permitted now; it's proper for us both to do this to fulfil all God requires." Then John consented.

So Jesus was baptised. On coming up out of the water he was praying. At that moment the heavens were torn open and he saw the Holy Spirit descending, like a dove in appearance. It alighted on him and a voice came from heaven: "You are my Son, my darling; with you my plan for the salvation of mankind rests."

Then John gave this testimony: "I saw the Spirit come down from heaven as a dove which remained on him. I wouldn't have known him, except that the one who sent me to baptise with water said to me, 'He on whom you see the Spirit descend and remain is the one who will baptise with the Holy Spirit.' I've seen and therefore I testify that this is the Son of God."

Tempting alternatives

Then Jesus, full of the Holy Spirit, returned from the Jordan and was led by the Spirit into the wilderness. He was in the wilderness, with wild animals, being constantly tempted by Satan. After fasting for forty days and forty nights, he was famished. Then Satan, the Tempter, came to him and said, "If you really are the Son of God, command these stones to become little loaves of bread."

Jesus answered him, "It's written: 'Man doesn't live by bread alone, but on every word that issues from the mouth of God.'"

Then Satan (*also known as the Devil*) took him to the holy city, Jerusalem, and had him stand on the tallest temple turret. "If you really are the Son of God," he said, "throw yourself down from here. Because it's written:

'He will give orders to his angels concerning you, to protect you and they will lift you up in their hands in case you strike your foot against a stone.'"

Jesus answered him, "It's also written: 'Don't put the Lord your God to the test.'"

Then the Devil took him again, this time, to a very high mountain. In a moment he showed Jesus all the kingdoms of the world in all their splendour. "I'll give you all this authority and splendour, because it's been given to me, and I can give it to whomever I please," he said, "if you will bow down and worship me."

Jesus said to him, "Be gone from me, Satan! It's written: 'You shall worship the Lord your God, and serve him only.'"

When the Devil had tried every type of temptation, he left until another opportune time. Then angels came and took care of Jesus.

First followers

The next day, with two of his disciples, John was standing by the Jordan. When he saw Jesus walking by, he said, "Look, the Lamb of God!"

The disciples heard him say this so they followed Jesus. Turning around, Jesus saw them following and asked, "What are you looking for?"

They said, "Rabbi (which means 'Teacher'), where are you staying?"

"Come," he replied, "and you'll see."

So they went, saw where he was staying, and spent the remains of the day with him since it was about four in the afternoon.

One of the two who had heard John speak, and who had followed Jesus, was Andrew. The first thing he did was to find his brother Simon and tell him, "We've found the Messiah". Then he led him to Jesus.

Jesus looked at Simon and said, "So you're Simon, son of John. You'll be called Peter" (which, means Rocky).

The next day Jesus decided to go to Galilee.

He found Philip and said to him, "Follow me."

Philip, like Andrew and Peter, was from the town of Bethsaida. Philip found Nathanael and said to him, "We've found the one Moses wrote about in the Law, and about whom the prophets also wrote – Jesus, the son of Joseph, from Nazareth."

"Nazareth! Can anything good come out of there?" Nathanael retorted. "Come and see for yourself," said Philip. When Jesus saw

Nathanael approaching, he said about him, "Here's a genuine Israelite, in whom there's no deceit." "How do you know me?" Nathanael asked.

Jesus answered, "Before Philip called you, I saw you while you were still under the fig tree."

Then Nathanael declared, "Rabbi, you really are the Son of God; you are the King of Israel."

Jesus replied, "You believe – simply because I told you I saw you under the fig tree? You'll see greater things than that." He continued, "I tell you the truth, you'll see heaven opened, and the angels of God ascending and descending on the Son of Man."

Jesus had returned to Galilee in the power of the Spirit, and rumours about him spread throughout the surrounding countryside. He taught in synagogues, and was praised by everyone.

Now Jesus was about thirty years old when he began his ministry. It was supposed that he was the son of Joseph.

One day Jesus was walking along the shore of the *Sea of Galilee*[9]. People started to crowd around him. So he stood and they listened to the word of God. Then he noticed, at the water's edge, two boats left there by the fishermen who were washing the boats and preparing their nets for casting into the lake. He went aboard one of the boats (which belonged to Simon, called Peter), and asked him to row out a little from the shore. He then sat down and taught the crowd from the boat.

When he had finished speaking, he said to Simon, "Put out into deep water, and you – let down your nets for a catch."

Simon answered, "Master, we wore ourselves out throughout the night and caught nothing. Nevertheless, because it's you that's saying it, I'll let down the nets."

Having done this, they caught such an enormous number of fish that their nets began to tear. So they beckoned their partners, James and John, the sons of Zebedee, in the other boat, to come and help them. They came and filled both boats so full that they were almost foundering.

When he saw what had happened, Simon Peter flung himself down at Jesus' knees and said, "Leave me, Lord; I'm a wayward man!" He and all his crew were astonished at the catch of fish they had taken – and so were James and John.

Then Jesus said to Simon, "Stop being fearful; from now on you'll be catching people for LIFE". Turning to Simon and Andrew he said, "Come, follow me, and I'll train you to fish for folk." At once they pulled their boats onto the shore, left their nets, abandoning everything, and followed him.

Going on a little farther, he saw the two other brothers, James and John. They were now in a boat with their father Zebedee. Straightaway Jesus called them, immediately they left their father in the boat with the hired hands and followed him.

First sign – 100% proof

Two days later there was a wedding at Cana in Galilee. Jesus' mother was there, and Jesus had been invited also, along with his disciples. When the wine ran out, Jesus' mother said to him, "They've no more wine."

"Dear mother, your concern and mine aren't the same", Jesus replied. "My time hasn't come yet."

However his mother said to the servants, "Do whatever he tells you."

Nearby were six stone jars, each with a capacity of twenty to thirty gallons (approx. 90-130 litres each), which were used for ceremonial washing.

Jesus said to the servants, "Fill the jars with water." So they filled them to the brim.

Then he said to them, "Now draw some out and take it to the chief steward."

They did so, and the chief steward tasted the water that had become wine. He did not know where it had come from, although the servants who had drawn the water knew. Then he called the bridegroom and said, "Everyone serves the good wine first then the inferior wine after the guests have had too much to drink; but you've saved the best wine until now."

This miracle was the first of the signs which Jesus performed that revealed his glory, and his disciples began to put their faith in him.

After this he went down to Capernaum – with his mother and brothers and his disciples. There they remained for a few days.

To Jerusalem…

It was almost time for the Passover, so Jesus went up to Jerusalem.

While he was in Jerusalem at the Passover Feast, many people saw the miracles he performed and believed in him. But Jesus did not entrust himself to them, because he knew all people. He did not need someone to tell him what people are like, because he understood human nature.

First explanations

Now there was a man named Nicodemus, a Pharisee and member of the Judean *ruling council*[10]. He came to Jesus secretly, during the night, and said, "Rabbi, we know you are a teacher who has come from God. No-one would be able to do these signs you are doing unless God were with him."

Jesus answered him, "The absolute truth is that, unless someone is born from above, they aren't able to perceive the kingdom of God."

"How can a man be born when he is old?" Nicodemus asked.

"Surely he's not able to enter a second time into his mother's womb to be born!"

Jesus answered, "The honest truth is that unless someone is born of water and the Spirit they're unable to enter the kingdom of God. Flesh gives birth to flesh, but the Spirit gives birth to spirit. So why wonder at my saying, 'You must be born from above'? The wind blows wherever it wants. You hear it's sound, but you don't know where it comes from nor where it's going. It's like that with everyone who is born of the Spirit."

"How is it possible for these things to happen?" Nicodemus asked.

"You're a teacher of Israel," said Jesus, "yet you don't understand these things? The honest truth is that we speak of what we know, and we testify to what we've seen, but you still don't accept our testimony. If I've told you of earthly things but you don't believe; how can you believe if I tell you of heavenly things?

No-one has ever gone into heaven except the one who came from heaven – the Son of Man.

And just as Moses lifted up the snake in the wilderness, so it's necessary for the Son of Man to be lifted up, in order that everyone who believes in him may have *everlasting life*[11]. You see this is how much God LOVES the people of the world; he gave his unique darling Son, so that everyone who believes in him will not be alienated (from him for ever) but will have eternal life.

God didn't send his son into the world that he might judge its people, but in order to save them through faith in him. Whoever believes in him isn't judged, but whoever doesn't believe stands judged already because he hasn't believed in the name of God's darling son.

This is the verdict: Light has come into the world, but people loved darkness instead of light because their deeds were evil. Everyone who practises evil hates the light, and won't come into the light for fear that their deeds will be exposed. But whoever is living by the truth comes into the light, so that it may be clearly revealed that what he has done has been done through God."

John steps back

After the festival, Jesus and his disciples went out into the Judean countryside, where he spent some time with them, and baptised people. The Pharisees heard that Jesus was making and baptising more disciples than John, although in fact it was not Jesus who baptised, but only his disciples.

John was also baptising at Aenon near Salim, as water was plentiful there. So people kept coming to be baptised.

A dispute developed between some of John's disciples and certain Judeans, over the matter of purification rites. They came to John and said to him, "Rabbi, the man who was with you on the other side of the Jordan – the one you testified about – look, he's baptising, and everyone is going to him."

To this John replied, "A man can't receive anything unless it's given him from heaven. You yourselves witnessed that I said, 'I'm not the Messiah but am sent ahead of him.' The bride belongs to the bridegroom. The friend of the bridegroom waits and listens for him, and joyfully rejoices when he hears the bridegroom's voice. This joy is mine, and it's now complete. It's necessary now for him to increase and for me to decrease.

The one who comes from above is above all; the one who is from the earth belongs to the earth, and speaks about earthly things. The one who comes from heaven is greater than all. He testifies to what he has seen and heard, yet no-one receives his testimony. The man who has accepted it has certified that God is truthful. The one whom God has sent speaks the words of God, because God gives to him the Spirit without limit. The Father LOVES the Son and has given everything into his hands. Whoever believes in the Son has *eternal life,* but whoever disobeys the Son won't see life, for God's judgement remains on him."

John imprisoned

When John reproved Herod because of Herodias, his brother's wife, and all the other evil things that Herod had done, Herod added this to the list: he locked John up in prison.

When Jesus heard that John had been arrested and imprisoned, he left Judea and returned once more to Galilee.

PART 2

The Wonder Years
&
The Clash of Kingdoms

CHAPTER 3

Good News Travels

Living water

To reach Galilee Jesus felt compelled to pass through Samaria. So
he came to a town in Samaria called Sychar, near the plot of ground
which Jacob had given to his son Joseph. One of Jacob's wells was
there, so Jesus, weary from the journey, sat down by the well. It was
about midday so his disciples had gone into the town to buy food.

Then a woman came to draw water. Jesus said to her, "Give me
a drink." The woman said to him, "How can you, being a Judean
man, ask me, a Samaritan woman, for a drink?" (Judeans wouldn't
use the same utensils as Samaritans – ever!)

Jesus answered her, "If you only knew the opportunity God is
giving you and who it is that asks you for a drink, you'd have asked
him and he would have given you living water."

"Sir," the woman said, "you haven't a bucket to draw water and
the well is deep. Where can you get this living water from? Surely
you can't be greater than our forefather Jacob who gave us the well
and drank from it himself, as did his sons and his cattle?"

Jesus answered her, "Whoever drinks this water will be thirsty
again; but whoever drinks the water which I give will never ever be
thirsty. Indeed, the water I give him will turn into a fountain of water
welling up within him into everlasting life."

The woman said to him, "Sir, give me this water so that I won't
be thirsty and have to keep coming here to draw it up."

He told her, "Go, call your husband and come back here." "I don't have a husband", she replied.

Jesus said to her, "You did well to say, 'I've no husband'. The fact is you've had five husbands, and the man you are living with now certainly isn't your husband. So what you've said is quite true."

"Sir," the woman said, "I see you're a prophet. Our forefathers made this mountain a place of worship, but you Judeans say that Jerusalem is the place where one should worship…"

"Believe me, woman," Jesus replied, "a time is coming when you'll worship the Father neither on this mountain nor in Jerusalem. You people worship what you don't understand; we worship what we do understand, because salvation comes from the Judeans. But a time is coming – and has now come – when the genuine worshippers will be those who worship the Father in Spirit and truth. Indeed, these are the kind of worshippers the Father is seeking. God is Spirit, and those who worship him must worship him in Spirit and in truth."

The woman said to him, "I know that The King is coming. When he comes, he'll explain everything to us."

Jesus said to her, "I am he, the one who is talking to you."

Right at that moment his disciples returned and they were astonished to find him talking with a woman. But no-one asked, 'What are you looking for?' or 'Why are you speaking to her?'

Then, leaving behind her water-pot, the woman went back into the town, where she said to the people, "Come and see a man who told me everything I've ever done. Might he not be the Messiah?" So the people came out of the town and made their way towards him.

In the meantime his disciples urged him, "Master, eat something."

But he said to them, "I've food to eat that you know nothing about."

So his disciples said to one another, "Surely no-one has brought him anything to eat?"

"My food," said Jesus, "is to do the will of him who sent me and to finish his work. Don't you have a saying, 'Four months more and then the harvest comes'? I tell you, open your eyes and look at the fields! They're white now, ready for harvest. Already the reaper is receiving his wages; even now he gathers fruit for eternal life, in order that the sower and the reaper may be glad together. Thus the saying is true, 'One sows, another reaps'. I sent you to reap what you haven't worked for. Others have done the hard work, but you've reaped the benefits of their labour."

Many Samaritans from that town believed in him because of the woman's testimony, 'He told me everything I've ever done'. When the Samaritans came to him they urged him to stay with them. So he remained there two days and, because of his words, many more became believers. They said to the woman, "We no longer believe because of what you said. But now, because we've heard for ourselves, we know that this man really is the Saviour of the world."

Good news

After those two days he left for Galilee. When he arrived there he publicly proclaimed, "The times are changing; the kingdom of God is near. Change your mind and heart, turn from your former life and believe the good news!" The Galileans welcomed him because they too had gone to Jerusalem and had seen all that he had done during the Feast.

Another vital sign

Once again Jesus went to Cana, where he had turned the water into wine. When a certain court official from Capernaum, whose son was ill and about to die, heard that Jesus had returned from Judea, he went to him and asked him to come down to his house and cure his son. "Unless you see miraculous signs and wonders," Jesus told him, "you'll never believe." The official persisted saying, "Lord, come down before my child dies."

Jesus replied, "Go on your way. Your son lives."

The man believed the word Jesus had spoken to him and departed. While he was going home his servants met him with the news that his child was alive and well. He inquired of them as to the time when his son had recovered, and they said to him, "The fever left him yesterday afternoon, at one o'clock." The father realised that was exactly the same time that Jesus had said to him, 'Your son lives'. So he and his entire household became believers.

This was now the second miraculous sign that Jesus did in Galilee, having returned from Judea.

Rejected at Nazareth

One day he went to Nazareth, where he had been brought up. On the *Sabbath*[12] day he went into the *synagogue*[13], as was his custom. He stood up to read, and the scroll of Isaiah was handed to him. After unrolling it, he found the place where it is written:

'The Spirit of the Lord is on me; he has anointed me to preach good news to the poor. He has sent me to proclaim release for the captives and recovery of sight for the blind, to bring freedom to the oppressed and to proclaim the year of the Lord's favour.'

After reading this he rolled up the scroll, gave it back to the attendant and sat down – (*in Messiah's chair!*) The eyes of everyone in the synagogue were focused on him. Then he began to speak to them saying, "Today, in your hearing, this scripture has been fulfilled."

Everyone protested; they were amazed that he had quoted only the gracious words (and omitted the words about God's vengeance). "Isn't this Joseph's boy?" they demanded.

Jesus said to them, "No doubt you'll say, 'What we've heard that you did in Capernaum, do here in your home town also'. You'll even quote this proverb to me, 'Physician, heal yourself!' But it's true to say," he continued, "no prophet is accepted in his home town. I tell you that there were many widows here in Israel, in Elijah's day, when there was no rain for three and a half years and there was a severe famine throughout the land. Yet Elijah wasn't sent to any one of them, but only to a widow living in Zarephath, in the region of Sidon. Also there were many in Israel with leprosy during the time of Elisha the prophet, yet not one of them was cleansed – except Naaman from Syria."

When they heard this, all the people in the synagogue were furious. They rose up and drove him out of the town, manoeuvring him to the top of the hill on which the town was built, in order to fling him over the cliff. But he walked right through the crowd and went on his way.

Amazement in Capernaum

Jesus left Nazareth and went to live in Capernaum, a town in Galilee which was by the lake in the area of Zebulun and Naphtali.
[This fulfilled what was said through the prophet Isaiah:
'Land of Zebulun and land of Naphtali, towards the (Mediterranean) Sea, beyond the Jordan, Galilee of the Gentiles[14] – the people living in darkness have seen a great light; on those living in the land of the shadow of death a light has dawned.']
When the Sabbath came, Jesus went into the synagogue and began to teach. The people were astonished at his teaching, because he was teaching as one who has authority, not like the teachers of the law.

In the synagogue there was a man possessed by a demon, an unclean spirit. Suddenly he cried out at the top of his voice, "Ha!

Jesus of Nazareth, what's there in common between you and us? Have you come to destroy us? I know who you are – the Holy One of God!"

"Shut your mouth!" said Jesus sternly, "and come out of him at once!" The spirit convulsed the man violently and threw him down before them all; then, with a shriek, came out of him, without doing him any harm.

The people were all so amazed that it became a general topic of conversation. They kept asking each other, "What's this new teaching? With authority and power he gives orders to evil spirits and they obey him!"

News about him spread quickly throughout the surrounding area and the whole region of Galilee.

Mother-in-law healed

As soon as he left the synagogue, he went with James and John to the home of Simon Peter and Andrew. Simon's mother-in-law had been lying in bed for some time, suffering with a high fever. Straightaway Jesus was told about her and was asked to help. So he went to her, bent over, took her hand and rebuked the fever. The fever left her; she got up at once and began to serve them.

Many more healed

That evening after sunset the people, in a constant procession, brought all their friends and relatives who had various kinds of ailments, and the demon-possessed, to Jesus. The whole town gathered at the door. Laying his hands on each one, he healed all the sick.

[This was fulfilling what was spoken through Isaiah: 'He took up our infirmities and carried our diseases.']

With only a word he evicted the spirits. Many came out shouting 'You are the Son of God!', but he rebuked them and wouldn't permit them to speak because they knew he was the Christ.

In the last watch of the night (*between 3 a.m. and 6 a.m.*), while it was still dark, Jesus got up, left the house and went to a solitary place, where he prayed. Simon and his companions went to look for him. When they had tracked him down, they exclaimed: "The whole world is looking for you!"

Jesus replied, "Let's go elsewhere – to the nearby villages – so I can take the good news there also. That's the reason why I've come."

The crowds came and tried to keep him from leaving them; but he said, "I must declare the good news of the kingdom of God to the other towns as well."

So Jesus travelled all around Galilee, teaching in the synagogues of Judea, preaching the good news of the kingdom, healing every disease and sickness among the people, and casting out demons.

Reports about him spread even throughout Syria. People brought to him all who were ill with various diseases, those suffering severe pain, the demon-possessed, those having seizures, and the paralysed; he healed them all. Great crowds from Galilee, the Ten Towns, Jerusalem, Judea and the region across the Jordan, followed him.

Leprosy healed

While Jesus was in one of the towns, an infectious man, who was in an advanced stage of leprosy, came along. When he saw Jesus he begged him, on his knees and with his face to the ground, saying, "Lord, if you're willing, you've power to make me clean."

Moved with compassion, Jesus reached out his hand and touched the man. "It's what I want," he said. "Be clean at once!" Immediately the leprosy left him and he was cured.

Then Jesus sent him away, sternly ordering him, "See that you don't tell this to anyone. But go and show yourself to the priest, and offer the sacrifices that Moses commanded as a proof of your cleansing."

Instead, the man went out and began to talk incessantly about it, spreading the news. Consequently, Jesus could no longer enter a town openly, so he stayed outside in remote places. Yet the news about him spread all the more, and crowds of people continued to come to him from everywhere to hear him and to be healed of their infirmities.

But Jesus often withdrew for a while to deserted places and prayed.

Paralysis healed

After some days, Jesus again entered his own town of Capernaum. The people heard that he had come home so an extraordinary number gathered, such that there was no room left, not even outside the door. As he was teaching and chatting about the things of God with them, Pharisees and teachers of the law, who had come from every village of Galilee, and from Judea and Jerusalem, were sitting there.

That day the power of the Spirit was in him to heal.

At that time several men arrived with a paralysed man. The man was lying prostrate on a mat being carried aloft by four of them. They tried to take him into the house to lay him before Jesus, but were unable to do so because of the crowd. So they went up on the roof and, after digging through the tiles, lowered him on his mat through the opening into the middle of the crowd, right in front of Jesus.

Seeing their faith, Jesus said warmly to the paralysed man, "Take heart; your sins are forgiven."

The Pharisees and teachers of the law were thinking to

themselves, 'Why does this fellow talk like that? He's blaspheming! Who can forgive sins except God alone?'

Immediately Jesus knew in his spirit that this was what they were thinking in their hearts, so he said to them, "Why are you thinking these things? Why do you entertain evil thoughts in your hearts? Which of the two is easier: to say to the paralysed man 'Your sins are forgiven', or to say 'Stand up, take your mat and start walking'? But in order that you may know beyond doubt that the Son of Man has authority on earth to forgive sins…" he said to the paralysed man, "I tell you, stand up, take your mat and go home." Instantly the man stood up, picked up his mat and walked out in full view of them all. He went home praising God.

When the crowd saw this, they were filled with awe, and praised God who had given such authority to men. They were saying "We've never seen anything like this; we've seen extraordinary things today!"

Levi leaves all

After this, Jesus strolled along the lakeside. As he was passing by he saw a *tax collector*[15] called Matthew, sitting at the customs office. "Follow me," Jesus told him. Matthew (also known as Levi, the son of Alphaeus) got up, left everything and followed him.

Then Matthew held a great banquet at his house. A large crowd of tax collectors and 'sinners' were reclining at the table with Jesus and his disciples, as there were many who followed him. But when the Pharisees, and some teachers of the law who subscribed to their beliefs, saw this they muttered to his disciples asking, "Why does your teacher eat and drink with tax collectors and the scum of society?"

On hearing this, Jesus answered them saying, "It's not the healthy who need a doctor, but the sick. Go and check out and learn what this scripture means, 'I desire mercy not sacrifice' because I've not come to call those who think they are all right, but the wayward."

CHAPTER 4

Rattling Religious Rules

Fasting habits

On one occasion John's disciples and the Pharisees were observing a fast. Some people came and asked Jesus, "How is it that John's disciples often fast and pray, and so do the disciples of the Pharisees, but yours carry on eating and drinking?"

Jesus answered, "How can the guests of the bridegroom fast and mourn while he is with them? They can't. But a time will come when the bridegroom will be taken away from them; then, in those days they'll fast."

He told them this parable: "No-one sews a patch of un-shrunken cloth on an old worn-out garment; otherwise the patch will pull away from the garment, making the tear worse. No-one tears a piece from a new coat and sews it on an old one. If they do, they'll have torn the new coat, and the patch from the new won't match the old. Again, no-one pours new wine into old wineskins, as the skins will burst, the wine will run out and both the wine and the wineskins will be ruined. No, they pour new wine into new wineskins, and both are preserved. No-one after drinking old wine wants the new, for they say, 'The old is good enough.'"

A Sabbath healing

Sometime later, Jesus went up to Jerusalem for a festival. Near the

Sheep Gate there is a pool called Bethesda that is surrounded by five covered porches. Here a large number of invalids used to lie – the blind, the lame, the paralysed – waiting for the waters to be disturbed.

(It was believed that from time to time an angel would come and stir the waters and that the first person to get into the pool when this happened would be cured of whatever disease they had.)

One man, who had been an invalid for 38 years, was lying there. When Jesus saw him, knowing that the man had been like that for a long time, he asked him, "Do you want to be well?"

"Sir," the man replied, "I've no-one to help me into the pool when the water is stirred. While I'm on my way, someone else always goes down ahead of me."

Jesus said to him, "Get up! Pick up your mat and walk." Immediately the man was healed; he took up his mat and began to walk around.

The day when this happened was a Sabbath, so the Judean religious leaders said to the man who had been healed, "It's the Sabbath; the law forbids you to carry your mat."

But the man answered, "The man who made me well, he said, 'Pick up your mat and walk.'"

So they asked him, "Who's this fellow who told you to pick it up and walk?"

The man did not know who it was as there had been a crowd in the place and Jesus had slipped away. Later Jesus found him in the temple and said to him, "See, you're well. Stop sinning or something worse might happen to you." The man went away and reported that it was Jesus who had made him well.

Those Judeans began persecuting Jesus because he was doing such things on the Sabbath. But addressing their objections, Jesus said, "My own Father is at work even on this very day, so I'm working too." For this reason they were more eager to kill him: not only was he breaking the Sabbath, but he was even calling God his own Father, thereby making himself equal with God.

Life in the Son

Continuing to answer them, Jesus said, "The honest truth is that the Son can't initiate anything himself. He does what he sees his Father doing. Whatever the Father does the Son does likewise. My Father is tenderly affectionate towards his Son and shows him all he does. Yes, and he'll show him even more marvellous works than these for you to wonder at. For example, the Father raises the dead and gives them LIFE, so the Son also gives LIFE to whomever he wants. The Father judges no-one, but has given all judgment to the Son so that everyone can honour the Son just as much as they honour the Father. The person who doesn't honour the Son doesn't honour the Father who sent him.

I'm telling you the truth: whoever hears my word and believes him who sent me has everlasting life and won't come under judgment; they've already been transferred out of death into LIFE. Mark my words, a time is coming – in fact it's already here – when the dead will hear the voice of the Son of God; and those who hear will live. You see just as the Father has LIFE in himself, he has made his Son the source of LIFE also. And because he is the Son of Man, the Father has given him authority to execute judgment.

Don't be surprised at this, because a time is coming when all the people who are dead will hear his voice and come out of their graves – those who've done good will rise to live again, and those who've done evil will rise to judgment.

I can do nothing on my own: as I hear, I judge, and my judgment is just, because I don't seek to please myself but him who sent me. Neither do I receive human honour because I know that you don't have the love for God within you. I've come in my Father's name, yet you don't receive me; but if another person comes in his own name, you'll receive him. How can you believe if you receive honour from one another, yet make no effort to obtain the honour that comes from God?"

Five witnesses to the claims of Jesus

Jesus continued: "If I alone testify about *myself*, my testimony is inadmissible.

But there's another person who testifies in my favour, and I know that his testimony about me is valid. You sent messengers to *John* who has testified to the truth. Not that I accept human testimony; but I mention this in order to help you to be saved. John certainly was a burning and shining lamp, whose light you chose to enjoy for a time.

Then I've a weightier witness than John's; *the works* which the Father has given me to finish and which I'm doing, testify that the Father has sent me.

Also *the Father* himself has testified on my behalf. You've never heard his voice nor seen his shape, and his word isn't alive in you because you don't believe the one he sent.

You scrutinise *the Scriptures* because you think that in them you have eternal life. You're right, these are the very ones that testify about me, yet you don't want to come to me in order to have LIFE.

But don't think I'll accuse you before the Father. Your accuser is Moses, in whom you've set your hopes. If you believed Moses, you'd believe me because he wrote about me. But if you don't believe his writings, how will you believe my words?

Hasn't Moses given you the law? Yet not one of you keeps it. Why, for example, are you seeking to kill me?"

"You are demon-possessed," a voice in the crowd answered. "Who's trying to kill you?"

Jesus said to them, "I did one miracle, and everyone marvelled. Yet, because Moses gave you circumcision (though actually it didn't come from Moses, but from the patriarchs), you circumcise a child on the Sabbath. Now if a child can be circumcised on the Sabbath so that the Law of Moses won't be broken, why are you angry with me for making an entire man whole on the Sabbath? Stop judging according to appearances, but judge each case fairly."

After the festival Jesus returned to Galilee...
A Sabbath stroll

On the following Sabbath Jesus made a detour through some cornfields. His disciples, being hungry, began plucking off some ears of grain. They rubbed the grain in their hands then ate the kernels. When the Pharisees saw this, they said to him, "Look! Why are your disciples doing what's unlawful on the Sabbath?"

Jesus answered them, "Have you never read what David did when he and his men were hungry and in need? He entered the house of God when Abiathar was high priest, and, taking the consecrated bread, he ate what legally only the priests could eat. He also gave some to his companions. Or haven't you read in the Law that on the Sabbath the priests in the temple desecrate the day and yet are innocent? I tell you that one greater than the temple is here. If you had known what these words mean, 'I desire mercy, not sacrifice,' you wouldn't have condemned the innocent."

Then Jesus said to them, "The Sabbath rest was made for humanity, not humanity for your Sabbath rules. So man is master even of the Sabbath."

Another Sabbath confrontation

Having moved on from that place, on another Sabbath day, Jesus went into a synagogue. A man was there whose right hand was shrivelled. Jesus was teaching,

The Pharisees and the teachers of the law were also there, spying on Jesus, looking for an excuse to bring a formal accusation against him. They watched him closely and asked, "Is it lawful to heal on the Sabbath?"

But Jesus knew what they were thinking and said to the man with the shrivelled hand, "Get up and stand in front of everyone." So he got up and stood there. Then Jesus said to them, "If any of you has a sheep and it falls into a pit on the Sabbath, wouldn't you grab hold of it and lift it out? How much more valuable is a human being than a sheep! I ask you, which is lawful on the Sabbath: to do good or to do evil, to save life or to destroy it?"

They remained silent.

Jesus looked around at each of them, his eyes blazing in anger and, deeply distressed at their stubborn hearts, he said to the man, "Stretch out your hand." The man did so and his hand was completely restored just as sound as the other.

Yet the Pharisees were furious; they went out to discuss with one another what they might do to Jesus. They began to conspire with the pro-Herod party about how they might kill him.

Healing the crowds

Aware of this, Jesus, with his disciples, withdrew to the lake. An exceptionally large crowd from Galilee followed him; and he healed all their sick.

When people heard about all that Jesus was continually doing, a great number came to him from all over Judea, Jerusalem, Idumea, the regions across the Jordan and around the coast of Tyre and Sidon. There was now a large company of his disciples. Because of all the people and to prevent the crowd from crushing him, Jesus told his disciples to keep a small boat always ready for him.

Jesus had healed so many people, that those with distressing diseases were pushing forward, jostling to touch him because power was coming from him and healing them all. Whenever evil spirits saw him, the demonised flung themselves down in front of him and cried out, "You, yes you, you're the Son of God." But Jesus repeatedly insisted and gave strict orders to them not to reveal who he was.

[This fulfilled what was spoken through the prophet Isaiah:
'Here is my servant whom I have chosen, the one I love, in whom I delight;

I will put my Spirit on him, and to the nations he will proclaim justice.

He will not quarrel nor cry out; and in the streets no-one will hear his voice.

A bruised reed he will not break, and a smouldering wick he will not snuff out,

till he leads justice to victory. In his name the nations will put their hope.]

Appointing apprentice apostles

About that time, Jesus went up onto a mountainside to pray. He spent the night praying. When morning came, he called his disciples to him and chose and appointed twelve of them, whom he also designated apostles – to be his constant companions, so that he might send them out as his ambassadors to preach and have authority to drive out demons.

These are the twelve he appointed:

Simon (to whom he gave the nickname *Peter*) and his brother *Andrew, James,* a son of Zebedee, and his brother *John* (to them he gave the nickname 'Boanerges', which means 'Sons of Thunder'), *Philip, Bartholomew, Matthew, Thomas, James* son of Alphaeus, *Thaddaeus* (also known as Judas, son of James), *Simon* the Zealot, and *Judas of Kerioth.*

CHAPTER 5

Teaching The Way[16]

Blessings and woes

Having seen the crowds, Jesus returned to the mountainside and sat down where there was a level place. His followers came to him; taking a deep breath he turned to them and began to teach saying:

"Blessed are those of you who are poor in spirit: yours is the kingdom of heaven.

Blessed are those who mourn and weep now: they'll laugh and be comforted.

Blessed are those with gentle spirits: they'll inherit the earth.

Blessed are those of you who hunger and thirst for righteousness: you'll be filled and satisfied.

Blessed are those who are merciful: they'll be shown mercy.

Blessed are the pure in heart: they'll see God.

Blessed are the peacemakers: they'll be called sons of God.

Blessed are those who are persecuted for doing what's right: theirs is the kingdom of heaven.

Blessed are you when people insult you, hate you, persecute you, exclude you, tell lies and say all kinds of evil things against you because of your commitment to me. Rejoice and be glad in that day and leap for joy, because they persecuted the prophets who lived before you in the same way. And great is your reward in heaven.

But, woe betide you who are rich now: you've already received your comfort in full.

Woe betide you who are well fed now: you'll go hungry.

Woe betide you who are self-satisfied now: you'll mourn and weep.

Woe betide you when everyone speaks well of you, for that's what their fathers did to the false prophets."

Salt and light

"You're the salt of the earth. Salt is good, but if it loses its characteristic qualities, how can it be made salty again? It is no longer good for anything, even for the soil or manure heap. It's fit only to be thrown out and trampled on.

You're the light of the world. A city built on top of a hill can't be concealed. Do people light a lamp to hide it in a basket or put it under a bed or in the cellar? No! Instead, they put it on a stand so that everyone who comes into the house can see by its light. In the same way, let your light shine, so that people will see your good deeds and praise your Father in heaven."

Beyond legal obligations

"Don't come to the conclusion that I've come to abolish the Law or the Prophets; I haven't come to abolish them but to fulfil them. I tell you the truth, until heaven and earth pass away, not a single letter or the smallest dot will pass from the Law until everything is fulfilled. Whoever relaxes one of the least of these commandments, and teaches others to do the same, will be called least in the kingdom of heaven. But whoever practises and teaches these commands will be called great in the kingdom of heaven. I tell you, that unless your righteousness goes beyond that of the Pharisees and the teachers of the law, you will never enter the kingdom of heaven.

You've heard that it was said to our forefathers, 'Don't commit murder, because anyone who commits murder will be brought before the court.' But I say to you that anyone who is angry with his brother will be liable to judgment.

Again, anyone who insults his brother is answerable to the Sanhedrin and anyone who says, 'You moron!' will be in danger of the fire of hell.

You've heard that it was said, 'Don't commit adultery.' But I say to you that anyone who looks at someone with a lustful desire has, in their heart, already committed adultery with them.

If your right eye leads you astray, gouge it out and throw it away. It's better for you to enter LIFE in the kingdom of God one-eyed than to have two eyes and be thrown into the fire of hell.

Again, you've heard that it was said to former generations, 'Don't break your vows, but keep the vows you've made to the Lord.'

But I say to you, don't accompany what you say with an oath at all: neither by heaven, because it's God's throne; nor by the earth, because it's his footstool; nor by Jerusalem – it's the city of the Great King. And don't swear by your head, because you can't make one hair white or black. Let what you say be simply 'Yes' or 'No'; anything beyond these is worthless.

You've heard that it was said, 'An eye for eye, and a tooth for a tooth.'

But I say to you, don't resist an evil person. If someone punches you on the right jaw, turn the other to him also. If someone wants to sue you and take your shirt, let him have your coat as well. If someone forces you to go one mile, go with him two. Don't turn away from anyone who asks you to give, or who wants to borrow from you. If anyone takes what belongs to you, don't demand it back.

You've heard that it was said, 'LOVE your neighbour and hate your enemy.'

But I say to you: LOVE your enemies, do good to those who hate you, keep praying for those who mistreat you and persecute you. Bless those who curse you so that you may be sons of your Father in heaven. He causes his sun to rise on the evil and the good; he sends rain on the just and the unjust. If you love those who love you, what credit is that to you, what reward will you receive? Even the tax collectors and the wayward are doing that! If you greet only your brothers, is that so very out-of-the-ordinary? Even people from other nations do that; don't they? If you do good to those who are good to you, what credit is that to you? Even the wayward do that. If you only lend to those from whom you expect repayment, what credit is that to you? Even the wayward lend to each other expecting to be repaid in full. But you – lend without expecting to receive anything in return, then your reward will be great, and you'll be sons of the Most High, because he's kind to the ungrateful and the wicked.

Be compassionate, therefore, even as your heavenly Father is compassionate.

Do to others as you'd have them do to you.

This sums up the Law and the Prophets."

Judgment, forgiveness & reconciliation

"Don't judge others, or you too will be judged in the same way. Don't condemn others, and you'll not be condemned. Forgive, and you'll be forgiven.

If you forgive when people commit offences against you, your heavenly Father will also forgive you. But if you don't forgive people their offences, your Father won't forgive yours.

Why don't you judge for yourselves what's right? As you're going to the magistrate, with your adversary, be minded to settle matters quickly while you're on the road. Try hard to be reconciled or they may drag you off to a judge who may turn you over to the court official, who will throw you into prison. I tell you, you won't be released until you've paid the last penny.

If you're bringing your gift to the altar and then remember that your brother has something against you; leave your gift there by the altar. Go and first be reconciled to your brother; then come and offer your gift.

Why do you pay attention to the splinter of wood in another person's eye but fail to see the plank in your own? How can you say, 'Let me take the splinter out of your eye,' when you pay no attention at all to the plank in your own? You hypocrite, first take the plank out of your own eye, and then you'll see clearly to remove the splinter from the other person's eye."

He told them a parable: "Can a blind man guide a blind man? Won't they both fall into a pit?"

Good and bad fruit

"Beware of false prophets who come to you in sheep's clothing, but inwardly are ravenous wolves. Just like a tree, you'll recognise them by their fruit. Do people pick figs from thorn bushes, or grapes from thistles? No! Every good tree bears good fruit, but a bad tree bears bad fruit. A good tree can't produce rotten fruit, and a rotten tree can't produce good fruit. Every tree that doesn't produce good fruit is cut down and thrown into the fire.

Likewise, a good person brings good things out of the good stored up in their heart, but the evil person brings evil things out of the evil stored up in their heart; because a person speaks out of what fills their heart."

The narrow way

"Enter through the narrow gate. Wide is the gate and easy is the way that leads to destruction; many enter through it. But narrow is the gate and restricted is the road that leads to LIFE; only a few find it.

Not everyone who says to me, 'Lord, Lord,' will enter the kingdom of heaven, but only those who do the will of my Father who's in heaven. Many will say to me on that day, 'Lord, Lord, didn't we prophesy in your name and in your name drive out demons and perform many mighty deeds?' Then I'll declare to them, 'I never knew you. Away from me, you evil doers!'"

Giving

"When you give to the needy, don't announce it with a fanfare, as the hypocrites do in the synagogues and on the streets, to be honoured by men. I tell you the truth; they've received their reward in full. But when you give to the needy, don't let your left hand know what your right hand is doing, so that your giving may be in secret. Then your Father, who sees what's done in secret, will reward you. It's more blessed to give than to receive, so give and it will be given to you. A good measure, pressed down, shaken together and running over, will be poured into your lap. Pay attention to what you hear, because with the measure you use, it will be measured to you in return and still more will be added. To the one who has, more will be given and from the one who hasn't, even what they have will be taken away.

Don't give to hounds what's holy; don't throw your pearls to pigs. If you do, they may trample them under their feet, then turn and tear you to pieces.

Beware of doing your good deeds in front of other people, in order to be seen by them. Otherwise you'll have no reward from your Father in heaven."

Fasting

"Whenever you fast, don't scowl like the gloomy hypocrites –

they disfigure their faces to show they're fasting. Truthfully speaking; they've already received their reward in full. But when you fast, freshen yourself up, so that it will not be obvious to others that you're fasting, but only to your Father, who's unseen; then your Father, who sees what's done in secret, will reward you."

Praying

"Whenever you pray, don't be like the hypocrites; in order to be seen, they love to pray standing in the synagogues and on street corners. Truthfully speaking, they've already received their reward in full. But when you pray, go into your private room, and having shut the door, pray to your Father who's unseen; then your Father who sees what's done in secret, will reward you.

Also, when you pray, don't keep on babbling as people from other faiths do; they think they'll be heard because of their many words. Don't be like them, because your Father knows what you need before you ask him."

Where the heart is

"Don't store up for yourselves treasures on earth, where moth and rust destroy, and where thieves break in and steal. Rather, store up for yourselves treasures in heaven, where neither moth nor rust can destroy, and where thieves don't break in and steal. Where your treasure is, there your heart will be also.

No one can keep on serving two masters. Either they'll hate the one and love the other, or they'll be devoted to one and despise the other. You can't continue serving God and Money."

Doing

"Why do you call me 'Lord, Lord' but don't do what I say?

I'll show you what the person is like who comes to me and hears these words of mine and puts them into practice:

They can be compared to a wise man building a house. He dug down deep then laid the foundation on rock. When the rain came down, the rivers rose, a flood came and the winds blew and beat against that house, yet it didn't fall nor shake because it was well built with its foundation on rock.

However, the one who hears these words of mine but doesn't put them into practice can be compared to a foolish man who built his house, without a foundation, on sand. The rain came down, the rivers rose; the winds blew and beat against that house. Then, when the flood struck, the house collapsed – it was totally ruined."

The crowds were amazed at the teaching they had heard, because Jesus was teaching them as one who had authority, unlike their own teachers.

When he had finished saying all these things, Jesus came down from the mountainside and large crowds followed him.

CHAPTER 6

Belief and Unbelief

Sick slave saved

Jesus entered Capernaum. There, a young slave, highly valued by a centurion to whom he belonged, was sick and close to death. The centurion, having heard about Jesus, sent some Judean elders to represent him and beg Jesus to come and save his slave. When they came to Jesus, they pleaded earnestly with him, "Lord this man deserves to have his request granted, because he loves our nation and has himself built the synagogue for us. His slave is bedridden in the house, he's paralysed and suffering terribly."

So Jesus went with them saying, "I'll go and heal him."

He was not far from the house when the centurion sent friends to say to him, "Lord, don't trouble yourself further, I'm not worthy to have you under my roof. That's why I didn't even presume to come to you myself. But just speak the word now, and my slave will be healed. I also am a man who's been placed under authority, with soldiers under me. I command this one, 'Go!' and he goes; and to another 'Come!' and he comes; and to my slave, 'Do this!' and he does it."

When Jesus heard this, he was amazed and turning to the people who were following him said, "I'm telling you the truth, I haven't found such great faith in anyone in Israel. I'm telling you, many will come from the east and the west, and will eat at the table with Abraham, Isaac and Jacob in the kingdom of heaven. But the intended heirs of the kingdom will be thrown outside, into the darkness, where there'll be weeping and gnashing of teeth."

Then Jesus said, "Go! Let it be done just as you've believed." At that very moment the slave was healed. The men who had been sent, returned to the house and found the slave well.

Dead son raised

Soon afterwards, Jesus went to a town called Nain. His disciples travelled along with him, accompanied by a large crowd. As he approached the town gate, a man's body was being carried out to be buried. His mother was a widow and this was her only son. A considerable crowd from the town was with her. When the Lord saw her, his heart went out to her and he said, "Don't cry."

Then he went and touched the bier; the pallbearers stood still. He said, "Young man, I am speaking to you, get up!" Immediately the dead man sat up and began to talk! Jesus then gave him back to his mother.

Everyone was filled with awe and praised God saying, "The Great Prophet has appeared among us; God has visited his people."

This news about Jesus spread throughout Judea and the surrounding countryside.

John's doubts

All these things were reported to John (the Baptiser) by his disciples while he was in prison. On hearing what Jesus was doing, he summoned two of his own disciples and sent them to the Lord to ask him, "Are you the 'One who is coming', or should we expect someone else?"

Having found Jesus the men said, "John sent us to you to ask 'are you the 'One who is coming' or should we expect another?'"

At that time Jesus was healing many people of diseases, sicknesses and evil spirits, and giving sight to many who were blind. So he replied to the messengers, "Go back and report to John what you've heard and seen: The blind receive sight, the lame walk, those who have leprosy are cured, the deaf hear, the dead are raised, and the good news is being preached to the poor. Blessed is the man who's not offended by me."

Jesus honours John

After John's messengers left, Jesus began to speak to the crowd about John. "What did you go out into the wilderness to look at? A reed being shaken by the wind? A man dressed in designer clothes? No, those wearing expensive clothing and living in luxury are in palaces. Then what did you go out to see? A prophet? Yes, I tell you, and more than a prophet. This is the one about whom it is written:

'Look, I am sending my messenger ahead of you, who'll prepare your highway for you.'

Truthfully speaking, among those who have ever been born there hasn't arisen anyone greater than John the Baptiser; yet the one who's least in the kingdom of heaven is greater than he. From the days of John the Baptiser until now, the good news of the kingdom of heaven has been preached and has been powerfully advancing, and forceful folk are laying hold of it. All the Prophets and the Law prophesied until John, and if you're willing to accept it, he's the Elijah who was to come. Now think carefully about what you have heard."

(When all the people, including the tax collectors, heard these words, they acknowledged that this was God's plan, since they had been baptised by John. But the Pharisees and teachers of the law rejected God's purpose for them, because they had not been baptised by John.)

Jesus continued...

"To what, then, can I compare the people of this generation? What are they like?

They're like children sitting in the marketplace and calling out to one another:

'We played the flute for you, but you didn't dance;

we sang a dirge, but you didn't cry'

Because John the Baptiser came neither eating cake nor drinking wine you said, 'He has a demon.' Now the Son of Man has come – eating and drinking – and you say, 'Look! a glutton and a drunkard, a friend of tax collectors and the wayward.' However God's wisdom is vindicated by its fruit."

Unbelieving towns

Then Jesus took the opportunity to reproach the towns in which the majority of his miracles had been performed, because they did not repent. "Alas for you, Chorazin! Alas for you, Bethsaida! If the miracles that were performed in you had been performed in Tyre and Sidon, they'd have repented long ago, in sackcloth and ashes. I tell you, it'll be more bearable for Tyre and Sidon on the Day of Judgment than for you. And you, Capernaum, will you be exalted to heaven? No, you'll be brought down as far as Hades. If the miracles that were performed in you had been performed in Sodom, it would have remained to this day. But I tell you that it'll be more bearable for Sodom on the Day of Judgment than for you."

A gate-crasher's faith

One of the Pharisees kept on inviting Jesus to come and eat with him, so one day Jesus went to the Pharisee's house and reclined[17] at the table. When a woman, who had been a prostitute in that town, learned that Jesus was eating in the Pharisee's house, she went along as well, bringing an alabaster jar of perfume. As she stood behind him, weeping, she began to wet his feet with her tears. Then she stooped down and wiped them with her hair and continued kissing them and anointing them with the perfume.

When the Pharisee, who had invited him, saw this, he said to himself, 'If this man were a prophet, he'd perceive who's touching him and what sort of woman she is – that she's a sinner.'

Jesus, aware of his thinking, answered him, "Simon, I've something to say to you."

"Go on teacher," he said.

"Two men owed money to a certain moneylender. One owed him five hundred pounds, and the other fifty. Neither of them had the money to pay him back, so he freely forgave the debts of both. Now which of them will love him more?"

Simon replied condescendingly, "I suppose the one who was forgiven the bigger debt."

"You've judged correctly", Jesus said.

Then turning towards the woman he said to Simon, "Do you see this woman? I entered your house; you gave me no water for my feet, but she wet my feet with her tears and wiped them with her hair. You didn't give me a kiss, but this dear woman, from the time I entered, hasn't stopped kissing my feet. You didn't anoint my head with oil, but she has poured expensive perfume on my feet. Therefore, I tell you, her sins which were many, have been forgiven – for she loved much. But the person who has been forgiven little loves little."

Then Jesus said to her, "Your sins are forgiven."

The others reclining at the table began murmuring among themselves, "Who on earth is this who thinks even he can forgive sins?"

Jesus said to the woman, "Your faith has saved you; go in peace."

Free and liberal women

After this, Jesus continued to travel around from one town and village to another, proclaiming the good news of the kingdom of God. The Twelve were with him, also some women who had been cured of evil spirits and diseases: Mary (of Magdala) from whom Jesus had cast out seven demons; Joanna the wife of Cuza, the steward of Herod's household; Susanna; and many others. Out of their own resources, these women were supporting Jesus and the Twelve.

Family pressure

Then Jesus entered a house; again a crowd gathered, so that he and his disciples were not even able to eat. When his family heard about this, they said, "He's out of his mind." So they went to take charge of him.

While Jesus was still talking to the crowd, who were sitting in a circle around him, his mother and brothers arrived and stood outside, wanting to speak to him, but they were not able to get near him because of the crowd. They sent someone in to tell him, "Your mother and brothers are outside asking to speak to you."

Jesus replied to him asking, "Who is my mother, and who are my brothers?" He looked at those around him and, gesturing towards his disciples, said, "Here are my mother and my brothers! Whoever hears God's words and puts them into practice, thereby doing the will of my Father in heaven, is my brother and sister and mother."

False accusation

A demonised man, who was blind and mute, was brought to Jesus so Jesus healed him. Once the demon had left, the man could both talk and see. The crowd was amazed and said, "Nothing has ever been seen like this in Israel; could this be the Son of David?"

But when the Pharisees and the teachers of the law, who had come down from Jerusalem, heard this they said, "He has an evil spirit, he's possessed by *Beelzebub!*[18] It's only by the prince of demons that this fellow casts out demons."

Jesus, knowing their thoughts, spoke to them in parables saying, "How's it possible for Satan to drive out Satan? If a kingdom is divided against itself, that kingdom is ruined and can't stand. If a household or city is divided against itself, that household or city won't stand. If Satan has risen up against himself, he's divided and his end has come. How then can his kingdom stand? And if you claim that I drive out demons by Beelzebub, by whom do your people drive them out? Therefore, they'll be your judges. But if I drive out demons by the Spirit of God, then the kingdom of God has arrived among you.

When a strong man, fully armed, guards his own house, his possessions are safe. How can anyone enter and ransack his house and carry off his possessions unless he first ties up the strong man? But when someone stronger attacks and overpowers him, he takes away the armour in which the man trusted, then he can plunder his house and divide the spoils.

Whoever isn't with me is against me, whoever doesn't gather with me, scatters. Therefore I tell you, people will be forgiven for every sin and blasphemy, except that whoever maliciously represents the Holy Spirit will never be forgiven – they're guilty of an eternal sin.

Anyone who speaks a word against the Son of Man will be forgiven, but anyone who blasphemes the Holy Spirit will not be forgiven, neither in this age nor in the age to come."

(He said this because they kept on saying he was possessed by an evil spirit.)

You brood of vipers! How can you who are evil say anything

good? I tell you that, on the Day of Judgment, people will have to give an account for every careless word they've spoken. By your own words you'll be acquitted, and by your own words you'll be condemned."

Demand for a sign

Then some of the Pharisees and teachers of the law said to him, "Teacher, we demand to see a miraculous sign from you."

He answered, "An evil and unfaithful generation demands a miraculous sign! But none will be given it except the sign of the prophet Jonah. Just as Jonah was three days and three nights in the belly of a sea monster, so the Son of Man will be three days and three nights in the heart of the earth. The people of Nineveh will stand up at the judgment with this generation and condemn it; for they repented at the preaching of Jonah; now someone much greater than Jonah is here. At the judgment, the Queen of the South will rise with this generation and condemn it; she came from the ends of the earth to listen to Solomon's wisdom; now someone much greater than Solomon is here.

When an evil spirit comes out of a person, it goes through arid places seeking rest but doesn't find it. Then it says, 'I'll return to my house which I left.' When it arrives, it finds the house standing empty, swept clean and put in order. Then it goes and takes along seven other spirits more wicked than itself, they go in and take up residence there. So the final condition of that person is worse than the first. That's the way it will be with this evil generation."

CHAPTER 7

Kingdom Parables

The sown seed

Jesus went out of the house, sat by the lake and again began to teach. People were coming to Jesus from town after town. Such a huge crowd gathered around him that he climbed into a boat and sat in it out on the lake, while all the people stood facing him on the shore along the water's edge.

Then he taught them many things, mostly by means of parables, "Listen!" he said. "A farmer went out to sow his seed. It happened that as he was scattering the seed, some fell along the path – where it was trampled on and the birds came and gobbled it up. Some seed fell on ground full of rocks, where it didn't have much depth of soil – so it sprang up quickly, because the soil was shallow; but when the sun came up, the plants were scorched; they withered because they had neither root nor moisture. Other seed fell among thorn seeds – which grew up and utterly choked the plants so that they didn't bear grain. Still other seed fell on fertile soil – where it grew and kept on yielding a crop – multiplying thirty, sixty, or even a hundred times what was sown.

Now think carefully about what you've heard."

Why Parables?

When the crowd had left and Jesus was alone, The Twelve along with other followers approached him and began to question him about the parables, "Why do you speak to the people in parables?" they asked.

He replied, "The knowledge of the mysteries of the kingdom of God has been granted to you, but not to others. This is the reason why I speak everything in parables to those on the outside.

Indeed the prophecy of Isaiah is being fulfilled in them:

'You'll keep on hearing but you'll never understand;

You'll keep on seeing but you'll never perceive.

Because the heart of this people has become scared,

they scarcely hear with their ears, and their eyes they have closed.

Otherwise they might see with their eyes, hear with their ears,

understand with their hearts

and turn and be forgiven, then I would heal them!'

But blessed are your eyes because they see, and your ears because they hear. Truthfully, I tell you, many prophets and righteous men longed to see what you see and to hear what you hear, but never did."

A word of explanation

His disciples then asked him what this parable meant. Jesus said to them, "Don't you understand this parable? Then how on earth can you grasp any of the parables? Now, listen again to the parable of the farmer:

The seed is the word of God, the farmer sows the word.

Some people are like the path along which the seed is sown. They hear the message about the kingdom but don't fully understand it. Straightaway Satan comes and snatches away what was sown in their heart so that they may not believe and be saved.

Others are like the rocky places: they hear the word and at once receive it with joy, believing for a while, but they have no depth for roots to grow. They last only a short time as in the time of testing, when trouble or persecution comes because of the word, they quickly fall away.

Those who received the seed that fell among the thorns are those who hear the word, but as they go on their way, the stresses of life, the lure of riches and pleasures, and the desire for other things come in and choke the word so they don't produce any mature fruit.

But the seed that fell on fertile soil represents those of excellent character who hear the word, receive it, retain it, understand it and, by persevering, persistently produce a crop; yielding thirty, sixty or even a hundred times what was sown."

Kingdom growth – seeds & weeds

He also said, "This is what the kingdom of God is like. A man scatters seed on the ground. Night and day, whether he is asleep or awake, the seed sprouts and grows, though he himself doesn't know how. All by itself the soil produces grain – first the stalk, then the head, then the full kernel in the head. As soon as the grain is ripe, he puts in the sickle, because the harvest stands ready."

Jesus presented them with another parable: "The kingdom of heaven can be compared to a man who sowed good seed in his field. But while everyone was sleeping, his enemy came and sowed weeds among the wheat, then went away. When the wheat came up and formed grain, the weeds also appeared.

The land owner's servants came to him and said, 'Sir, didn't you sow good seed in your field? So how come it has weeds?'

'An enemy has done this,' he replied.

The servants asked him, 'Do you want us to go and pull them up now?'

'No,' he answered, 'because while you're pulling up the weeds, you may uproot the wheat as well. Let them both grow together until the harvest. At that time I'll tell the reapers, 'First gather the weeds and tie them in bundles to be burned; then gather the wheat into my barn.'"'"

He told them yet another parable: "The kingdom of heaven is like a grain of mustard seed, which a man took and sowed in his field. Although it is smaller than all other seeds you plant in the ground, when planted it grows and becomes the largest of all garden plants – a tree, so that the birds of the air can come and nest in the shade of its big branches."

Jesus spoke all these things to the crowd, and with many similar parables he spoke to them; according to what they could understand. He was not in the habit of saying anything to them without using parables, so fulfilling what was spoken through the prophet:

'I will open my mouth in parables; I will utter things hidden since the creation of the world.'

But privately, with his own disciples, he explained everything.

He left the crowd and went into the house. His disciples came to him and said, "Explain to us the parable of the weeds in the field."

He answered saying, "The one who sowed the good seed is the Son of Man. The field is the world, and the good seed are the children of the kingdom. The weeds are the offspring of the evil one, the enemy who sows them is the Devil. The harvest time is the end of this present age, the reapers are angels.

Therefore, just as the weeds are pulled up and burned in the fire, so it will be at the end of the age: the Son of Man will send out his angels, they will weed out of his kingdom everything that causes people to stumble, and all who are lawless and they will throw them into the fiery furnace, where there'll be weeping and gnashing of teeth. Then, in the kingdom of their Father, the righteous will shine out like the sun.

Now think carefully about what you've heard."

More kingdom parables…

"The kingdom of heaven is like yeast that a woman took and mixed into three measures of flour until it worked all through the dough."

"The kingdom of heaven is like treasure hidden in a field, which a man found and hid again, then in his joy he went and sold all he had and bought that field."

"Again, the kingdom of heaven is like a merchant looking out for pearls of rare quality. When he found one of great value, he went away and sold everything he had, then bought it."

"Or again, the kingdom of heaven is like a fishing-net that was cast into the lake and caught all kinds of fish. When the net was full, the fishermen pulled it up onto the beach. Then they sat down and collected the good quality fish into baskets, but threw away the bad. This is how it will be at the end of the age. The angels will come and separate the wicked from amongst the righteous and throw them into the fiery furnace, where there'll be weeping and gnashing of teeth."

"Have you understood all these things?" Jesus asked.

"Yes," they replied.

"So you see," he said to them, "every teacher of the law who's been instructed about the kingdom of heaven is like the head of a household who brings out of his storeroom new treasures as well as old."

When Jesus had finished these parables, he moved on from there.

CHAPTER 8

Kingdom Power

Jesus stills a storm

One day Jesus had a crowd around him. As evening came, he said to his disciples, "Let's go across to the other side of the lake."

So, Jesus, having dismissed the people, was taken, just as he was, aboard a boat, under the care of the disciples. They left the crowd behind, although other little boats accompanied them.

While they were sailing, Jesus fell asleep in the stern, with his head on a leather cushion. Then, without warning, a furious storm, with hurricane strength winds, came down on the lake, so that the waves washed over the boat, nearly swamping it. They were in great danger but Jesus was still sleeping. The desperate disciples went and woke him, yelling, "Lord, Master, save us! We're perishing! Don't you care?"

He awoke and rebuked the wind and the raging waters saying; "Quiet! Be still!"

Then the wind eased, the storm subsided and all was completely calm.

He asked his disciples, "Why are you so afraid? Do you still have no faith?"

Terrified, in fear and amazement the men asked one another "Who on earth is this? He commands even the winds and the waves, and they obey him!"

Jesus delivers the demonised

They sailed across the lake to the region of the *Gadarenes*[19], opposite Galilee. When they arrived at the other side, Jesus got out of the boat. As he stepped ashore, a demon-possessed man, from the town, came running to meet him.

For a long time this man had neither been fully clothed, nor had he lived in a house. He had been driven by the demons into solitary places and had made his home among the tombs. Many times the demons had seized him. Although he was chained hand and foot and had been kept under guard, he had broken his chains in pieces. No one could restrain him anymore; no one was strong enough to subdue him. Night and day among the tombs and in the hills he was continually screaming and shrieking and cutting himself all over his body with stones. He was so violent that no-one could pass that way.

Having seen Jesus from a distance, the man cried out and ran and prostrated himself on the ground before him, worshipping him. Then, at the top of his voice, he shouted, "What do you want with me, Jesus, Son of the Most High God? Have you come here to torture me before the appointed time? I beg you, don't torture me!"

Jesus kept asking, "What's your name?" The man replied, "My name is Legion, because there's many of us here."

Then repeatedly the demons begged Jesus not to order them to go into the Abyss.

A short distance away, on the nearby hillside, a large herd of pigs was feeding.

The demons begged Jesus, saying, "As you intend to cast us out, let us go into them."

Jesus gave them permission saying, "Come out of this man, you evil spirits!"

So they came out of the man and went into the pigs. The whole herd, about two thousand in number, rushed in a frenzy down the steep cliff into the lake and drowned. Those tending the pigs fled and reported this, including what had happened to the demon-possessed man, in the town and neighbouring farms. Then the whole town dashed out to see for themselves what had taken place.

When the townsfolk came to Jesus, they saw the man who had been possessed by the legion of demons, sitting there at Jesus' feet, dressed and in his right mind; and they were afraid.

Those who had witnessed this event told, in detail, how the demon-possessed man had been cured and what had happened to the pigs. Then all the people begged Jesus to leave their region because they were overcome with great fear. So he boarded the boat and left.

As Jesus was going on board, the man, who had been set free, begged to go with him. But Jesus sent him away, saying, "Go, return home to your family and tell them how much the Lord has done for you, and how he has had mercy on you." So the man went away and he began to proclaim publicly in the Ten Towns the great things Jesus had done for him. And all the people were amazed.

Jesus defeats disease and death

When Jesus had crossed to the other side of the lake, a large crowd welcomed him, since they were all expecting him. They gathered and pressed around him. Then, seeing Jesus, one of the synagogue rulers, a man named Jairus, who had an only daughter, came and knelt before him and pleading earnestly said, "My little daughter is dying. Please come to my house and lay your hands on her so that she shall be healed and live." So Jesus went with him, as did his disciples.

While Jesus was on his way, the crowds that followed almost crushed him. In the crowd was a woman who, for twelve years, had been subject to bouts of haemorrhaging. She had suffered a great deal under the care of many doctors and had spent all she had on them. Yet instead of getting better she got worse. No-one could cure her. When she heard about Jesus, she had kept saying to herself, "If I touch only the fringe of his garment, I'll be healed."

So she came up behind him and touched the edge of his cloak. Immediately her bleeding stopped and she felt in her body that she was freed from her suffering.

At once Jesus realised that power had gone out from him. He turned around in the crowd and asked, "Who touched me? Who touched my clothes?"

When they all denied it, Peter said, "Master, the crowd is jostling you, yet you can ask, 'Who touched me?'"

But Jesus would not be deterred, he said, "Someone did touch me; I know that power has gone out from me." So he kept looking around to see who had deliberately reached out to him in faith.

Then the woman, realising that she could not escape being noticed, and knowing what had happened to her, came trembling and fell at Jesus' feet. In the presence of all the people, she told him the whole truth why she had touched him and how she had been healed instantly. Then Jesus turned and said to her, "Take heart daughter, your faith has saved you. Go in peace and be freed from your affliction." From that moment the woman was fully restored.

While Jesus was still speaking, some men came from Jairus's house. "Your daughter's dead," they said. "Don't trouble the teacher anymore."

Overhearing what they said, Jesus said to Jairus, "Don't be afraid; keep trusting in me and she'll be saved."

When he arrived at the house he did not let anyone go in with him except Peter, James and John and the child's father and mother.

When he entered the house he saw flute players and people weeping and wailing loudly. He said to them, "Why all this commotion? Stop wailing! Go, the child isn't dead but asleep."

But they jeered at him, knowing that she had definitely died.

After throwing the crowd outside, he went into where the child was. He took the girl by the hand, and said to her, "Little girl, I say to you, awake!" Immediately her spirit returned. She stood up and walked around (she was twelve years old). Her parents were completely astonished. Then Jesus told them to give her something to eat and he gave strict orders not to let anyone know what had happened. However news of this spread through that entire region.

Jesus restores sight

As Jesus went on from there, two blind men followed him, calling out, "Have mercy on us, Son of David!"

After he had gone indoors, the blind men came to him. Jesus asked them, "Do you believe that I can to do this?"

"Yes, Lord," they replied.

Then he touched their eyes and said, "According to your faith let it be done to you." Their sight was restored immediately. Jesus warned them sternly, "See that nobody knows about this." But they went out and, all around that region, spread the wonderful news about him.

Jesus returns to Nazareth

Jesus left there and, accompanied by his disciples, went to his home town. When the Sabbath came, he began to teach the people in their synagogue. Most who heard him were completely flabbergasted saying, "From where does this man acquire this wisdom and these miraculous powers? Isn't this the carpenter? Isn't this Mary's son, and aren't his brothers James, Joseph, Simon and Judas? Aren't all his sisters here among us?" So they took offence at him.

But Jesus said to them, "No prophet is rejected except in his home town, among his own relatives and in his own house."

So, dumfounded by their lack of faith, he could not do any miracles there, except lay his hands on a few sick people and heal them.

Jesus' compassion

Then Jesus went through all the towns and from village to village, teaching in their synagogues, preaching the good news of the kingdom and healing every disease and sickness. When he saw the crowds, he had gut-wrenching compassion for them, because they were harassed and helpless, like sheep without a shepherd.

He said to his disciples, "The harvest is plentiful but the workers are few. Therefore, earnestly ask the Lord of the harvest to send out workers into his harvest field."

CHAPTER 9

Training the Twelve

Jesus summoned to him the twelve disciples (whom he had designated apostles) and gave them power and authority to drive out all demons, and to cure every disease and sickness. Then he sent them out two by two, to preach the kingdom of God and to heal the sick.

These were his instructions:

"Don't go to the other nations nor enter any Samaritan town. Rather, go to the lost and alienated sheep of the house of Israel. As you go, proclaim the good news: 'The kingdom of heaven has come near.' Heal the sick, raise the dead, drive out demons and cleanse those who have leprosy. Don't make any charge; freely you've received, freely give.

"Take nothing for the journey except a walking stick. Don't acquire gold nor take along any silver or loose copper change in your belts; take no begging bag for the road, no bread nor extra tunic or sandals, because the worker is worth his keep.

"Whatever town or village you enter, enquire for some influential person and stay at their house until you leave that town for good. As you enter the home, speak blessing on it. If the home is hospitable let your peace rest there; if it isn't, let your peace return to you. If people won't welcome you or if they won't listen to your words, as a testimony against them, when you leave that town, shake the dust from off your feet. I tell you the truth; it will be more bearable for Sodom and Gomorrah on the Day of Judgment than for that town."

Preparing for persecution

"I'm sending you out like sheep among wolves. Therefore be as shrewd as serpents and as delicate as doves.

Be on your guard, people will hand you over to the local councils and flog you in their synagogues. On my account you'll be dragged before governors and kings to be witnesses to them and to the nations. But when they arrest you, don't be anxious about how you should defend yourself, neither worry about what to say, nor how to say it. At that very time the Holy Spirit will teach you and you'll be given what to say; because it won't be you speaking, but the Spirit of your Father speaking through you.

Brother will betray brother to death, and a father his child; children will rise up against their parents and have them put to death. Everyone will hate you because of me, but those who stand firm to the end will be saved. When you're persecuted in one place, flee to another. I tell you the truth, you won't finish going through the towns of Israel before the Son of Man comes.

An apprentice isn't above their teacher nor a servant above their master. It's sufficient for the apprentice, when he is fully trained, to be like their teacher, and the servant, like his master. If the head of the house has been called Beelzebub, how much more the members of the household!

So don't be afraid of those who betray, hate or persecute you. There's nothing concealed that won't be disclosed, nor secret that won't be made known. What I tell you in the darkness, speak in the daylight; what's whispered in your ear, proclaim from the roof tops. I tell you, my friends, don't be afraid of those who kill the body but can't kill the soul. I'll show you whom you should fear; rather, fear him who, after killing the body, has power to destroy you in hell. Yes, I tell you, fear him.

Aren't two sparrows sold for a penny or five sparrows sold for two pennies? Yet not one of them is forgotten by God. Not one of them will fall to the ground apart from the will of your Father.

Indeed, the very hairs of your head are all numbered. Don't be afraid; you're worth more than many sparrows.

Whoever confesses their allegiance to me in the presence of people, I'll also confess my allegiance to them in the presence of my Father and his angels in heaven. But whoever disowns me in the presence of people, I'll disown in the presence of my Father and the angels in heaven."

Paying the price

"I've come to bring fire on the earth; how I wish it were already kindled! I've a baptism to undergo; how distressed I am until it is completed! Don't think that I've come to bring peace to the earth. I didn't come to bring peace, but a sword and division. From now on there'll be five in one family divided against each other, three against two and two against three. My coming will cause a father to turn against his son and a son against his father; a mother against her daughter and a daughter against her mother; a daughter-in-law against her mother-in-law and a mother-in-law against her daughter-in-law. A person's enemies will be the members of their own household.

Anyone who loves their father or mother more than me isn't worthy of me; anyone who loves their son or daughter more than me isn't worthy of me. Anyone who doesn't take up their cross and follow me isn't worthy of me. Whoever finds their life will lose it, and whoever loses their life for my sake will find it. The one who receives you receives me, and the one who receives me receives the one who sent me. Anyone who receives a prophet because they're a prophet will receive a prophet's reward, and anyone who receives a righteous person because they're righteous will receive a righteous person's reward."

After Jesus had finished instructing The Twelve, they set out and went from village to village, preaching repentance and proclaiming the good news. Everywhere they drove out many demons. They anointed many sick people with oil and healed them.

Jesus went on to teach and preach in the towns of Galilee.

A prophet perishes

At that time Herod heard the reports about Jesus and all that was going on, as Jesus' name had become well known. He repeated to his servants what some people were saying, "This fellow is John the Baptiser who's been raised from the dead and that's why miraculous powers are at work in him."

Others were saying, "He's Elijah, who has re-appeared," still others claimed that one of the old prophets had come back to life.

But Herod was perplexed, he said, "I beheaded John. Who is this I hear such things about?" And he tried to see Jesus.

It must be explained that Herod himself had given orders to have John arrested. He had had him bound and put in prison, because of Herodias, his brother Philip's wife, whom he, Herod had married. John had been saying to Herod: "It is not lawful for you to have your brother's wife."

So Herodias nursed a grudge against John and wanted to kill him. But she was not able to, because Herod feared John and kept him out of harm's way, knowing him to be a righteous and holy man. Herod heard John, and he was greatly puzzled; yet he liked to keep listening to him. He was also afraid of the people, because they considered John to be a prophet.

Eventually the opportune time came. On his birthday, Herod gave a banquet for his high officials, his military commanders and the leading men of Galilee. When Herodias' own daughter came in and danced, she delighted Herod and his dinner guests, so much so that the king promised her with an oath, saying, "Ask me for anything you want, and I'll give it to you, even up to half my kingdom."

She went out and said to her mother, "What shall I ask for myself?"

"The head of John the Baptiser", she answered.

So at once, prompted by her mother, the girl hurried into the king with this request: "I want you to give me the head of John the Baptiser on a platter – right now!"

The king was greatly distressed, but because of his oath and his dinner guests, he did not have the nerve to refuse her. So immediately he sent one of his bodyguards with orders to bring John's head. The man went, beheaded John in the prison, and brought back his head on a platter. He presented it to the girl who carried it to her mother.

On hearing of this, John's disciples came and took his body and laid it in a tomb.

Then they went and told Jesus.

An impromptu picnic

When Jesus heard what had happened; he wanted to withdraw by boat to a solitary place. At that time the apostles returned, reporting to Jesus all they had done and taught. However, they did not even have a chance to eat because so many people were coming and going. So Jesus said to them, "Come with me by yourselves to a quiet place and take a little rest in privacy." They withdrew in a boat by themselves and crossed towards Bethsaida on the far shore of the Sea of Galilee.

But many people saw them leaving and realised where they were going. Because they saw the miraculous signs Jesus had performed in healing the sick, they ran around the shore, arriving ahead of them.

When Jesus landed and saw a large crowd, he was moved with compassion because they were like sheep without a shepherd. So he welcomed them and, going up on a hillside, sat down with his disciples. He began healing their sick and teaching them many things about the kingdom of God.

Late in the afternoon, The Twelve came to him and said, "This is a remote place, and it's already getting late. Send the people away, so they can go to the neighbouring farms and villages to find lodgings and buy themselves some food."

Jesus replied, "They don't need to go away. You give them something to eat."

He said to Philip, "Where shall we buy bread for these people to eat?" (He asked this only to test him, as he already had in mind what he was going to do.)

Philip answered him, "Eight months' wages wouldn't buy enough bread for each one to have a bite! Are we to go and spend that much on bread and give it to them to eat?"

"Well, how many loaves do you have?" he asked. "Go and see."

When they found out, another of his disciples, Andrew, spoke up, "Here's a boy with five small barley loaves and a couple of pickled fish, but how far will they go among so many?"

"Bring them here to me," Jesus said.

There was plenty of lush grass in that place so Jesus directed The Twelve to have all the people sit down to eat. The people sat down in groups of hundreds and fifties, giving the appearance of flower beds in a garden.

Then taking the five little loaves and the two small fish and looking up to heaven, Jesus gave thanks and broke the loaves. He kept giving pieces to the disciples, and the disciples kept giving them to the people, as much as they wanted.

When they had all had enough to eat and were satisfied, he said to his disciples, "Gather the pieces that are left over. Let nothing be wasted."

So they gathered them up, filling twelve hampers with the broken pieces of the loaves and fishes left over by those who had eaten.

The number of those who ate was about five thousand men, plus women and children.

The Passover Festival was near. So when the people saw the miraculous sign that Jesus did, they began to say, "Surely, this is The Prophet who's to come into the world."

Jesus, realising that they intended to come and make him king by force, immediately made his disciples board the boat and go on ahead of him to Capernaum, on the other side, while he dismissed the crowd. Later that evening he went further up the mountain by himself to pray.

Phantom of the lake

When it was dark, Jesus was there alone, but the boat was already a considerable distance from land, being buffeted by the waves because a strong wind was blowing and the waters were rough.

Sometime after three o'clock in the morning, Jesus saw the disciples still straining hard at the oars. The boat was now in the middle of the lake; they had rowed only three to three and a half miles with the wind against them.

Jesus went out, walking on the surface of the lake, wanting to go to their aid. When they all saw him they screamed out, terrified, because they thought he was a ghost.

But Jesus called to them and said: "Take it easy! It's only me. Don't be afraid."

"Lord, if it's you," Peter replied, "tell me to come to you on the water."

"Come," he said.

Then Peter clambered down from the boat and walked on the water towards Jesus. But when he looked at the storm he was afraid and, beginning to sink, cried out, "Lord, save me!"

Immediately Jesus reached out his hand and caught him. "You have little faith," he said, "why did you hesitate?"

When they climbed into the boat, the wind died down. Then

those who were in the boat worshipped Jesus saying, "Truly you are the Son of God."

They were utterly dumbfounded, but their hearts were dull; they had not even understood about the loaves.

Instantly the boat reached the shore where they were heading.

When they had crossed over, they landed at Gennesaret where they anchored. As soon as they left the boat, the people of that place recognised Jesus. Running, they sent the news to the entire surrounding region. People carried their sick on mats to wherever they heard he was.

Food for Life

The next day the crowd that had stayed on the opposite shore of the lake realised that only one boat had been there, and that Jesus hadn't boarded with his disciples, but they had gone off on their own. Then some other boats from Tiberias landed near the place where the people had eaten the bread. Once the crowd realised that neither Jesus nor his disciples were there, they boarded the small boats themselves and went to Capernaum searching for Jesus.

When they found him on the other side of the lake, they asked him, "Rabbi, when did you arrive?"

Jesus answered, "I'll tell you the truth; you're not looking for me because you understand the miraculous signs but because you ate as much bread as you could. Don't work for food that perishes, but for food that persists into eternity, which the Son of Man – he on whom God the Father has placed his seal of approval – will give you."

Later, while Jesus was teaching in the synagogue in Capernaum, they asked him, "What must we do to do the works God requires?"

Jesus replied, "This is the work of God: that you believe in the one he has sent."

Then they asked him, "So what sign will you give that we may see and believe you? What will you do? Our forefathers ate the manna in the desert; just as the scriptures say: 'He gave them bread from heaven to eat.'"

Jesus said to them, "Actually, it wasn't Moses who gave you bread from heaven, but my Father who is even now giving you the true bread from heaven. The bread of God is the One who comes from heaven and gives LIFE to the world."

"Sir," they said, "from now on always give us this sort of bread."

Then Jesus declared, "I am that bread of LIFE. Whoever comes to me will never go hungry, and whoever believes in me will never be thirsty again. But as I told you, you've seen me and still you don't believe. All whom the Father gives me will come to me, and whoever comes to me I'll never drive away. I've come from heaven, not to do my own will but to do the will of him who sent me. And this is the will of him who sent me; that I should lose nothing of all that he has given me, but raise them up at the last day. My Father's will is that everyone who looks to the Son and believes in him shall have everlasting life, and I'll raise them up at the last day."

At this the Judeans began murmuring about him because he said, "I am the bread that came from heaven." They were saying, "Isn't this Jesus, the son of Joseph, don't we know his father and mother? How come he's now saying, 'I came from heaven'?"

"Stop grumbling among yourselves," Jesus answered. "No-one can come to me unless the Father who sent me draws them. It's written in the Prophets: 'They'll all be taught by God.' Everyone who listens to the Father and learns from him comes to me. No-one has seen the Father except the one who is from God; only he has seen the Father. I tell you the honest truth; whoever believes has everlasting life. I am the bread of LIFE. Your forefathers ate the manna in the desert, yet they died. But here's the bread that comes from heaven, which one may eat and not die. I am the living bread that came from heaven. If anyone eats of this bread, he'll live forever. This bread is also my flesh, which I'll give for the LIFE of the world."

Then the Judeans began quarrelling among themselves, "How can this fellow give us his flesh to eat?"

Jesus said to them, "The honest truth is that unless you eat the flesh of the Son of Man and drink his blood, you've no LIFE in you. Whoever eats my flesh and drinks my blood has eternal life. My flesh is the true food and my blood is the true drink. Whoever eats my flesh and drinks my blood remains in me, and I in him. Just as the living Father sent me and I live through the Father, so the one who feeds on me will live through me. This is the bread that came from heaven. Your forefathers ate manna and died, but the one who feeds on this bread will live forever."

On hearing this, many of his disciples said, "This is an offensive teaching. Who can be expected to accept it?"

Aware that his disciples were complaining about this, Jesus said to them, "Does this offend you? What if you see the Son of Man ascend to where he was before! It's the Spirit who gives LIFE; the natural life counts for nothing. The words I've spoken to you are spirit and they are LIFE. Yet there are some of you who don't believe." (Jesus had known from the beginning which of them did not believe, and who would betray him.) He went on to say, "This is why I told you that no-one can come to me unless the Father has enabled him."

As a result of this, many of his disciples turned back and no longer followed him.

"You don't want to leave too, do you?" Jesus asked The Twelve.

Simon Peter answered him, "Lord, to whom shall we go? You alone have the words which speak of eternal life and we've come to believe and know for certain that you're the Holy One of God."

Then Jesus replied, "Haven't I chosen you, The Twelve? Yet one of you is a devil!" (He meant Judas of Kerioth, the son of Simon, who, though one of The Twelve, was later to betray him.)

CHAPTER 10

Custom and Practice

Wherever Jesus went – into villages, towns or the countryside – the sick were laid in the marketplaces. People kept on begging him to let them touch even the tassels on his cloak. All who reached out and touched him were healed.

Conflict over traditions

Then some Pharisees and teachers of the law, who had come from Jerusalem, gathered around Jesus. They saw some of his disciples eating bread with hands that were 'unclean', that is, unwashed. (The Pharisees and all those who practise Judaism do not eat unless they give their hands a meticulous ceremonial washing, carefully keeping to the tradition of the elders. When they come from the marketplace they do not eat unless they wash. They observe many other traditions, such as the washing of cups, wooden pitchers and copper kettles.) So they kept asking Jesus, "Why don't your disciples live according to the tradition of the elders instead of eating their food with 'unclean' hands?"

Jesus replied, "And why do you abandon the commandments of God for the sake of adhering to traditions devised by men? You've a fine way of constantly setting aside the commands of God in order to observe your own traditions! For example Moses said, 'Respect your father and your mother,' and, 'Anyone who reviles his father or mother must be put to death.' But as for you, you're saying that if a man says to his father or mother, 'Whatever help you might otherwise have received from me is now a gift devoted to God,' then you no longer permit him do anything for his parents. Thus you invalidate the authority of the word of God for the sake of the tradition that you've handed down. You do many things like that all the time. You hypocrites! Isaiah was absolutely accurate when he prophesied about you:

'These people honour me with their lips, but their hearts are far from me.

They worship me in vain; their teachings are but rules taught by men.'"

Clean and unclean

Jesus called the crowd to him again and said, "Listen to me, everyone, and understand this. There's nothing from outside a person that can make them 'unclean'. What goes into a person's mouth doesn't make them 'unclean.' Rather, it's what comes out of their mouth which makes them 'unclean.'"

After he had left the crowd and entered a house, his disciples came to him and asked "Do you know that the Pharisees were offended when they heard this?"

He replied, "Every plant that my heavenly Father hasn't planted will be pulled up by the roots. Leave them; they are blind guides".

Peter said, "Explain the parable to us."

"Are you also still so dull?" Jesus asked them. "Don't you see that nothing that enters a person from the outside can make them 'unclean'? That whatever enters the mouth goes into the stomach and then out of the body, it doesn't go into their heart? (In saying this, Jesus declared all foods 'clean'.) He went on, "But the things that keep coming out of the mouth come from the heart, and these make a person 'unclean'. For out of the heart come depraved thoughts, murder, adultery, sexual immorality, theft, false testimony, greed, malice, deceit, lewdness, envy, slander, pride and folly. All these pernicious things come from within, making a person 'unclean', but eating with unwashed hands doesn't make anyone 'unclean'."

The faith of an alien

Jesus left that place and went off to the region of Tyre and Sidon. He entered a house but did not want anyone to know about it. But it was impossible to keep his presence secret. In fact, as soon as she heard about him, a Greek woman (born in Syrian Phoenicia) from that area came to him, repeatedly crying out, "Son of David, have mercy on me! My little daughter is suffering terribly from demon-possession."

But Jesus did not answer her, not even a word. So his disciples came to him and urged him, "Send her away, she keeps yelling out after us."

He answered, "I was sent only to the lost sheep of the house of Israel."

But the woman came and fell at his feet and begged Jesus to drive the demon out of her daughter. "Lord, help me!" she said.

He replied, "First let the children eat all they want. It's not right to take the children's bread and toss it to their pet dogs."

"Yes, Lord," she said, "but even the little dogs under the table always eat the little crumbs the little children allow to fall from their master's table."

Then Jesus answered, "Dear woman, you've great faith! For such a reply, you may go. Your request is granted, the demon has gone from your daughter."

She went home. That very hour she found her little child lying quietly on her bed, healed and the demon gone.

Back to Galilee

Then Jesus left the vicinity of Tyre and went through Sidon, walking down to the Sea of Galilee and into the region of the Ten Towns. There some people brought to him a man who was deaf and had a speech impediment also. They begged Jesus to place his hands on the man.

After he took him aside from the crowd, in private, Jesus put his fingers into the man's ears. Then he spat and touched the man's tongue with his spittle. He looked up to heaven and with a deep sigh said to him, "Be opened!" At this, the man's ears were opened, his tongue was loosened and he began to speak clearly. Jesus commanded the people not to tell anyone. But the more he did so, the more they kept talking about it; they were completely and utterly flabbergasted.

"He does everything well," they said. "He even makes the deaf hear and the mute speak."

Another miraculous meal

About that time he went up on a hillside and sat down. Great crowds came to him, bringing the lame, the blind, the crippled, the mute and many others. They placed them at his feet; and he healed them. The people kept being amazed when they witnessed the mute speaking, the crippled healed, the lame walking and the blind seeing. And they kept praising the God of Israel.

Jesus called his disciples to him and said, "I've compassion for these people, my heart goes out to them; they've now been with me three days and have nothing to eat. If I send them home hungry, they'll faint on the way, because some of them have come a long distance."

His disciples answered, "But where could we get enough bread in this desolate place to satisfy such a crowd?"

"How many loaves of bread do you have?" Jesus asked.

"Seven," they replied, "and a few small fish."

Jesus commanded the crowd to sit on the ground. Then having taken the seven loaves and the fish and given thanks and blessed them, he broke them and kept giving them to the disciples to distribute among the people. Thus they served the crowd.

They all ate and were satisfied. Afterwards the disciples picked up seven basketfuls of broken pieces that were left over. The number of those present who ate was about four thousand men, besides women and children.

Sign seekers

After sending the crowd away, Jesus, with his disciples, climbed into the boat and went to the region of *Magadan*[20].

The Pharisees and Sadducees came out and began disputing with Jesus. To test him, they asked him to show them a sign from heaven.

Sighing deeply he said, "When evening comes, you say, 'It'll be fair weather, because the sky is red,' and in the morning, 'Today it'll be stormy, as the sky is red and threatening.' Again, when you see a cloud rising in the west, immediately you say, 'It's going to rain,' and it does. When the south wind blows, you say, 'It's going to be hot,' and it is. Hypocrites! You know how to interpret the appearance of the earth and sky, how is it that you don't know how to interpret the signs of the times? Why does this wicked and adulterous breed of men ask for a miraculous sign? Truthfully, I tell you no sign will be given to it except the sign of Jonah."

Having sent them away they re-embarked.

Warning about blind teachers

When they went across the lake, the disciples had completely forgotten to take bread, except for one loaf they had with them in the boat. "Always be discerning," Jesus warned them. "Be on your guard against the yeast of the Pharisees and Sadducees and that of the Herodians."

They discussed this among themselves and said, "It's because we didn't bring any bread."

Aware of their discussion, Jesus asked them, "You of little faith, why are you talking among yourselves about having no bread? Do you still not understand? Are your hearts hardened? Do you have eyes but fail to see, and ears but fail to hear? Don't you remember when I broke the five loaves for the five thousand? How many basketfuls of pieces did you pick up?"

"Twelve," they replied.

"Then when I broke the seven loaves for the four thousand, how many basketfuls of pieces did you gather?"

They answered, "Seven."

"How is it you don't understand that I wasn't talking to you about bread? Beware of the yeast of the Pharisees and Sadducees which is hypocrisy, because nothing is hidden that is meant to be disclosed; and nothing concealed will not be revealed or brought into the open. What you've said in the dark will be heard in the daylight, and what you've whispered in the ear in the inner rooms will be proclaimed from the roofs.

"Now think carefully about what you've heard."

Then they understood that he was not telling them to beware of the yeast used in bread, but to beware of the teaching of the Pharisees and Sadducees.

Seeing clearly

They came to Bethsaida. Some people brought a blind man and begged Jesus to touch him. He took the blind man by the hand and led him out of the village. When he had spat on the man's eyes and laid his hands on him, Jesus asked, "Do you see anything?"

He looked up and said, "I see men, but they look like trees walking about."

Once more Jesus laid his hands on the man's eyes. Then his eyes were opened, his sight was restored, and he saw everything clearly. Jesus sent him home, saying, "Don't even go into the village."

CHAPTER 11

Faith for the Future

Who on earth?

Jesus and his disciples went on to the villages in the region of Caesarea Philippi. On the way he kept quizzing them, "Who do the crowds say the Son of Man is? Who do people think I am?"

They replied, "Some say John the Baptiser; others say Elijah; and still others, Jeremiah or one of the prophets who has come back to life."

"But what about you?" he persisted. "Who do you, yourselves, consider me to be?"

Simon Peter answered, "You – you're the Messiah, the Son of the living God."

Jesus replied, "Blessed are you, Simon, son of Jonah, because this was not revealed to you by human reasoning, but by my Father in heaven. I'm telling you: you're Peter, and on this rock I'll build my church, and the gates of Hades won't have power against it. I'll give you the keys of the kingdom of heaven; whatever you have locked on earth will already have been locked in heaven, and whatever you un-lock on earth will have already been un-locked in heaven."

Then Jesus strictly ordered his disciples not to tell anybody that he was the Messiah.

One for all

From then on Jesus began to teach and explain to his disciples that it was necessary for him to go to Jerusalem and suffer many things at the hands of the elders, the chief priests and the teachers of the law. Having been thoroughly examined and found faultless he would still be rejected by them and be killed and on the third day he would be raised to life again.

He spoke quite frankly about this, so Peter took him aside and began to rebuke him, "God forbid it, Lord!" he said. "This'll never happen to you!"

But Jesus wheeled around, and having looked at his disciples, he rebuked Peter, then he said, "Get behind me, Satan! You're a stumbling block to me; you don't have a mind for the things of God, but the things of men."

All for one

Then he called the crowd to him along with all his disciples and said to them, "If anyone wants to become my follower, they must lose sight of themselves and their own interests and take up their cross daily, and accompany me on the same road. For whoever wants to save their life will lose it, but whoever forfeits their life for me and for the good news will save it. What profit is it for a person if they gain the whole world, yet forfeit their very self? Or what can a person give in exchange for their life? If anyone is ashamed of me and my words in this adulterous and sinful generation, the Son of Man will be ashamed of him when he comes. For the Son of Man is going to come in his Father's glory, with his angels. Then he will reward each person, according to what he has done."

Then Jesus repeated one of his frequent sayings, "Truthfully speaking, some who are standing here won't taste death before they see the kingdom of God come with power."

A night on a mount

About a week later Jesus took with him Peter, James and John, and led them up a high mountain, where they were all by themselves, to pray. While Jesus was praying, he was transfigured: the appearance of his face changed – it shone like the sun; his clothes became dazzling white, as bright as a flash of lightning, more than any washing powder on earth could whiten them. Suddenly two men in glorious splendour appeared. They were Moses and Elijah who were holding a conversation with Jesus; speaking about Jesus' own exodus, which he was about to bring to fulfilment in Jerusalem.

Peter and his companions had dozed off but having roused themselves they saw Jesus' glory and the two men standing with him.

Just as the men were parting, Peter blurted out, "Master, it's wonderful for us to be here. If you wish, let's put up three shelters – one for you, one for Moses and one for Elijah." (He did not know what to say, the disciples were so frightened.)

While Peter was still speaking, a cloud of light appeared and enveloped them all. The disciples were more afraid as they entered the cloud. Then a voice from the cloud said, "This is my Son, my darling one whom I have chosen; with him I am well pleased. Pay attention to him!"

When the disciples heard this, they fell facedown to the ground, terrified. After the voice had fallen silent, Jesus came and touched them. "Get up," he said. "Don't be afraid." When they looked around, they no longer saw anyone with them but saw Jesus himself, alone, as he was.

I will rise again

As they were coming down the mountain, Jesus instructed them, "Don't tell anyone about what you've seen until the Son of Man has been raised from the dead." So they faithfully kept this matter to themselves, and told no-one at that time what they had witnessed. But all the time they were discussing with one another, particularly about what 'rising from the dead' meant.

The disciples questioned him, "Why do the teachers of the law constantly say that Elijah must come first?"

Jesus replied, "It's true, Elijah does come first and restores all things. But I tell you, Elijah already came, and they didn't recognise him, but did to him everything they wanted."

Then the disciples understood that he was talking to them about John the Baptiser.

"In the same way", Jesus continued, "the Son of Man is about to suffer many things and be rejected, just as it's written about him."

Nothing is Impossible

The following day, when they had come down from the mountain, on coming to the other disciples, they saw a large crowd around them. The teachers of the law were wrangling with them. On seeing Jesus, all the people were overwhelmed with wonder and immediately ran to greet him.

"What are you arguing about?" he asked.

A man in the crowd called out, "Teacher, I beg you, look at my son, he's my only child. A spirit has robbed him of speech. Whenever it possesses him he suddenly screams; it throws him to the ground in convulsions so that he foams at the mouth, grinds his teeth and becomes rigid. It hardly ever leaves him, it's destroying him. I begged your disciples to cast it out, but they couldn't." The man approached Jesus and kneeling before him implored, "Lord, have mercy on my son, he's suffering dreadfully."

"O unbelieving and perverted generation," Jesus replied, "how long am I to stay with you? How much longer am I to put up with you? Bring the boy here to me."

So they brought him. When the spirit saw Jesus, it immediately threw the boy into a complete convulsion. Falling to the ground, he began rolling around and foaming at the mouth.

Jesus asked the boy's father, "How long has this been happening to him?"

"From childhood," he answered. "It has often thrown him into fire or water to destroy him. But if you can do anything, have compassion on us and help us."

"If you can!" exclaimed Jesus. "Everything's possible for the one who believes."

Immediately the boy's father cried out, "I do believe; help my weak faith!"

When Jesus saw that a crowd was running to the scene, he rebuked the evil spirit. "You deaf and mute spirit," he said, "I command you, come out of him and never enter him again."

The spirit shrieked, convulsed him violently and came out. The boy looked just like a corpse so that many said, 'He's dead'. But Jesus took a firm grip of his hand and lifted him up. He stood, healed from that moment; so Jesus gave him back to his father.

They were all amazed at the greatness of God; everyone was marvelling at all that Jesus did.

After Jesus had gone indoors, his disciples asked him privately, "Why couldn't we cast it out?"

He replied, "This sort can come out only by prayer and fasting. You've so little faith."

The apostles said, "Lord, increase our faith."

He replied, "Truthfully speaking, if you've faith the size of a grain of mustard seed, you could say to this mountain, 'Move from here to there' and it'll move; or to a mulberry tree, 'be uprooted and planted in the sea' and it would obey you. Nothing will be impossible for you."

They left there and passed through Galilee. Jesus did not want anyone to know where they were, because he was teaching his disciples. When they came together, with great emphasis, he said to them "Carefully listen to what I'm about to tell you. The Son of Man is going to be betrayed into the hands of men. They'll kill him and, having been put to death, on the third day he'll be raised to life." The disciples were greatly distressed but they didn't understand what he meant by this saying. It was hidden from them, so that they couldn't grasp it, and they were afraid to ask him.

Faith for present needs

After Jesus and his disciples arrived in Capernaum, the collectors of the half-shekel tax came to Peter and asked, "Doesn't your teacher pay the temple tax?" "Yes, he does," he replied.

When Peter came into the house, Jesus, anticipating him, spoke first asking, "What do you think Simon – the kings of the earth, from whom do they exact dues and taxes – from their own folk or from others?" "From others," Peter answered.

"Then the family is exempt," Jesus said to him. "But so that we won't offend them, go to the lake and cast a hook. Take the first fish you catch, open its mouth and you'll find a shekel. Take it and give it to them for my tax and yours."

A question of greatness

At that time an argument arose among the disciples as to which of them was the greatest. Being in the house, Jesus asked them, "What were you arguing about along the road?"

But they kept quiet. Later Jesus asked, "Who's the greatest in the kingdom of heaven?"

Sitting down, he called The Twelve and said, "If anyone wants to be first, they must be prepared to be the last of all and the servant of all." Then, knowing their inner thoughts, he called a little child and had him stand beside him. He said, "The honest truth is that unless you turn round and become like little children, you'll never enter the kingdom of heaven. Therefore, whoever humbles themself, until they're like this child, is the greatest in the kingdom of heaven. Because the one who's least among you all, is the greatest."

The next generation

Taking the child in his arms, he said to them, "Whoever receives a little child like this for my sake receives me; whoever receives me doesn't receive me but the one who sent me. If anyone places a small stumbling stone before one of these little ones who believes in me, causing them to go astray – it would be better for that person to have had a massive millstone hung round their neck and been thrown into in the depths of the sea to drown. So watch yourselves. See that you don't despise one of these little ones; because I tell you, their angels always see the face of my Father in heaven. He isn't willing that any of these little ones should be lost. If anyone gives even a cup of cold water to one of these little ones because they're my disciple, I tell you the truth, they'll certainly not lose their reward."

Having a future perspective

"Woe betide the world because of the things that cause people to stumble! Such things must come, but woe to the person through whom they come! If your right hand or your foot causes you to stumble, cut it off and throw it away. It's better for you to enter life maimed or lame than to have two hands or two feet and be thrown into the eternal fire of hell where Isaiah says 'their worm doesn't die, and the fire isn't quenched.'

Everyone will be tested by fire, so live a disciplined and consecrated life. Salt is good for preserving life, so have salt in yourselves, and always be at peace with one another."

"Master," said John, "we saw a certain individual driving out demons in your name so we tried to restrain him, because he wasn't one of us."

"Don't hinder him," Jesus said. "No-one who does a mighty work in my name can in the next breath speak ill about me. Whoever isn't against us is for us."

Future harmony and forgiveness

"If someone wrongs you, go and show them their fault, keeping it between the two of you alone. If they listen to you, you've regained the relationship. But if they won't listen, take one or two others along, so that every word spoken may be established by the mouth of two or three witnesses. If the person refuses to listen to them, tell it to the church. If the person refuses to listen even to the church, let them be to you like an unbeliever or an outsider.

Truthfully I tell you that whatever you prohibit on earth will have been prohibited in heaven, and whatever you liberate on earth will have been liberated in heaven."

Then Peter approached Jesus, asking, "Lord, how many times shall I forgive my brother when he harms me? As many as seven times?"

Jesus answered, "If your brother does harm, rebuke him, then if he repents, forgive him. If he harms you seven times in a day, and seven times comes back to you and says, 'I repent,' forgive him. But I tell you, not only seven times, but seventy-seven times.

Thus the kingdom of heaven can be likened to a king who wanted to settle accounts with his servants. As he began, a man who owed him ten thousand pounds was brought to him. Because the man wasn't able to repay, the master commanded that he, his wife, his children and all that he had be sold to repay the debt.

The servant fell prostrate before him. 'Be patient with me,' he pleaded, 'and I'll pay back everything.' The servant's master had compassion on him, forgave the debt and let him go.

But having gone out, that servant found one of his fellow servants, who owed him a hundred pounds. The man seized the fellow servant and began to throttle him. 'Pay back what you owe me!' he demanded.

His fellow servant fell down and begged him, 'Be patient with me, and I'll repay you.'

But the man was unwilling to do so. Instead, he went and had his fellow servant thrown into prison until he could pay the debt.

When the other servants saw what had taken place, they were deeply distressed and went and told their master everything that had happened.

Then the master called in the servant. 'You wicked servant,' he said, 'I forgave all that debt of yours because you begged me to. Shouldn't you have had mercy on your fellow servant just as I had on you?' In anger his master handed him over to the jailers to be tortured, until he could repay all he owed.

This is what my heavenly Father will also do to you unless, from your heart, you forgive your brother."

CHAPTER 12

Working Holidays

More family pressure

After this, Jesus limited his travels to Galilee, purposely staying away from Judea because the religious establishment there were seeking an opportunity to kill him.

As the time for *Feast of Tabernacles*[21] was approaching, his brothers said to him, "Leave here and go to Judea, so that your disciples there can also see the things you are doing. Surely nobody does things in secret if they want public recognition. If you're really doing these things, show yourself to the world." (At that time even his own brothers did not believe in him.)

Jesus responded, "The right time for me hasn't yet arrived; but one day is as good as another for you. The world can't hate you, but it hates me because my life and speech demonstrate that what it does is evil. You go up to the Feast. I'm not going up to this feast, because the right time for me hasn't yet come."

Having said this, he remained in Galilee.

Secret journey

However, after his brothers had gone, he also went, not publicly, but secretly.

At the Feast the Judeans were looking for him and asking, "Where is that man?"

Among the crowds there was discreet debate about him. Some said, "He's a good man." Others replied, "No, he deceives the people." Yet, for fear of the religious leaders, no one was saying anything about him openly.

Public preaching

About halfway through the Feast week Jesus went up to the temple and began to teach. The Judeans marvelled, asking, "How did this man acquire such scholarship without being schooled?"

Jesus answered, "My teaching isn't mine. It comes from him who sent me. If anyone wants to do God's will, he'll find out whether my teaching comes from God or whether it's something I made up myself. Those who speak on their own authority seek to gain honour for themselves, but he who seeks the honour of the one who sent him is genuine; there's nothing false about him."

At that point some of the people of Jerusalem began to ask, "Isn't this the man they're trying to kill? Here he is, speaking openly, and they're saying nothing to refute him. Perhaps the rulers really do realise that this man is the Messiah? But we know where this man comes from; whenever the Messiah comes, no-one will know where he's from."

So, while still teaching in the temple, Jesus exclaimed, "Yes, of course you know me, and you know where I'm from. I'm not here on my own account, but he who sent me is true. You don't know him, but I know him because I've come from him and he sent me."

Threats, promises, disputes

At that time, many from the crowd put their faith in him. They said, "When the Messiah comes, surely he won't do more signs than this man."

The Pharisees heard the crowd muttering such things about him so they, and the chief priests, sent temple guards to arrest him.

Jesus said, "I'm with you for only a little longer, then I'm going away to the one who sent me. You'll seek me but you won't find me however much you search; because where I am, you can't come."

The Judeans said to one another, "Where does this man intend to travel so that we can't find him? Surely he's not intending to go to our people scattered among the Greeks, and teach the Greeks themselves, is he? What does he mean when he says, 'You'll seek me, but you won't find me,' and 'where I am, you can't come'?"

On the last day, 'The Great Day' of the Feast, Jesus stood and exclaimed in a loud voice, "If anyone is thirsty, let him come to me and drink. As the Scripture says, streams of living water will flow from the innermost being of those believing in me." (He said this about the Spirit, whom those who believed in him were to receive. As yet the Spirit had not been given, since Jesus had not yet been glorified.)

Having heard these words, some of the crowd said, "This man really is The Prophet."

Others said, "He's definitely the Messiah."

But still others asked, "Surely the Messiah doesn't come from Galilee? Doesn't the Scripture say that the Messiah will be David's descendant and from Bethlehem, the town where David lived?" Thus, amongst the crowd, a division about him occurred.

At this moment the temple guards tried to arrest him; but no-one laid a hand on him, because his time had not yet come. Finally they went back to the chief priests and Pharisees, who asked them, "Why didn't you bring him in?"

"No-one ever spoke like this man does," the guards declared.

"You mean you've been deceived also?" the Pharisees retorted. "Is there a single one of the rulers or Pharisees who has believed in him? No! Yet this confused crowd, that knows nothing of the law, is bewitched."

Nicodemus, the one who had gone to Jesus previously, was one of their own number and he asked, "Is it our law to condemn someone without giving them a hearing first, to find out what they're doing?"

They asked sarcastically, "Are you from Galilee, also? Search the Scriptures and see that The Prophet doesn't arise from Galilee."

Then they each went to his own home, while Jesus went to the Mount of Olives.

Outrageous grace

Very early in the morning Jesus came again to the temple. All the people were flocking to him, so he sat down and began to teach them. Then the teachers of the law and the Pharisees led in a woman who had been caught in adultery. They stood her in the centre of the group and said to Jesus, "Teacher, this woman has been caught in the very act of adultery. In our law Moses commands us to stone such women. What do you say about it?"

They were using this as a trap, in the hope of bringing a charge against him.

But Jesus, having squatted down, started to write in the dust with his finger. When they kept on goading him, he straightened up and said to them, "The person among you who's without sin, let him be the first to throw a stone at her." Again he squatted down and wrote in the dust.

Then those who heard him began to go away one at a time, beginning with the older ones, until Jesus was left alone with the woman still standing there. Having stood up he asked her, "Dear woman, where are they? Did no-one condemn you?"

"No-one, Lord," she said.

"Then neither do I condemn you," Jesus declared. "Go. But from now on leave your life of sin."

I am the light of the world

Again Jesus spoke to the people, saying, "I am the light of the world. Whoever follows me will never walk in darkness, but will have the light of LIFE."

The Pharisees challenged him, "You're appearing as your own witness; your testimony isn't valid."

Jesus answered them, "Even if I testify about myself, my testimony is valid, because I know where I came from and where I'm going. But you've no idea where I come from nor where I'm going. You judge according to human reasoning; I don't judge anyone. Even if I do judge, my judgments are right because I'm not alone. I stand with the Father, who sent me. In your own Law it's written that the testimony of two witnesses is valid. I'm one who testifies for myself; my other witness is the Father, who sent me."

So they asked him, "Where's your father?"

"You know neither me nor my Father," Jesus replied. "If you knew me, you'd know my Father also."

He spoke these words while teaching openly in the temple near the treasury. Yet no-one arrested him, because his time had not yet come.

I am not from this world

Once more Jesus said to them, "I'm going away, and you'll seek me, but you'll die in your sin. Where I go, you can't come."

Therefore the Judeans were saying, "Surely he won't kill himself will he? Is that why he's saying, 'Where I go, you can't come'?"

But he continued, "You're from below: I'm from above. You're of this world: I'm not from this world. I told you that you'd die in your sins; if you don't believe that I'm the one I claim to be, you will indeed die in your sins."

"Who are you then?" they asked.

"Just what I've been telling you from the beginning," Jesus replied. "I've much to say in judgment of you. But he who sent me is reliable, and what I've heard from him I tell the world."

They did not understand that he had been speaking to them about his Father. So Jesus said, "When you've lifted up the Son of Man, then you'll know that I'm the one I claim to be and that I do nothing on my own but speak only what the Father has taught me. The one who sent me is with me; he hasn't left me alone, for I always do the things that are pleasing to him."

While he was saying these things, many put their faith in him.

True freedom

To the Judeans who had believed him, Jesus said, "If you continue living in my words, you really are my disciples. Then you'll know the truth, and the truth will set you free."

They answered him, "We're Abraham's descendants; we never have been enslaved by anyone. How can you say that we'll be set free?"

Jesus replied, "The truth is that everyone who commits sin is a slave to sin. A slave has no permanent place in the family, but a son belongs to it forever. So if the Son sets you free, you'll be free indeed.

I know you're Abraham's descendants. Yet you're ready to kill me, because there's no place in you for my word. I'm speaking to you about the things that I've seen in the Father's presence, but you do what you've heard from your father."

Who is your Father?

"Abraham is our father," they answered.

"If you were Abraham's children," said Jesus, "then you'd be doing the things Abraham did. As it is, you're seeking to kill me, a man who has told you the truth that he heard from God. Abraham didn't do such things. You're doing the things your own father does."

"We're not illegitimate children," they protested. "God is the only Father we have."

Jesus said to them, "If God really is your Father, you'd love me, for I came from God – now I'm here. I haven't come on my own accord, but he sent me. Why isn't my language clear to you? It's because you're unable to bear to hear what I say. You belong to your father, the devil, so you want to carry out your father's desires. He was a murderer from the beginning; not standing for the truth, for there's no truth in him. When he lies, he speaks his native language, for he's a liar and the father of lies. Yet because I tell the truth, you don't believe me! Can any of you discover any sin in me? If I'm telling the truth, why don't you believe me? Whoever belongs to God hears the words of God. The reason you don't hear is that you don't belong to God."

The Judeans answered him, "Aren't we right in saying that you're a Samaritan and are demon-possessed?"

"I don't have a demon," said Jesus, "but I honour my Father and you dishonour me. I'm not seeking glory for myself; but there's one who seeks it, and he's the judge. The truth is that if anyone keeps my word, he'll never ever see death, even in the future age."

At this the Judeans exclaimed, "Now we know that you're demon-possessed! Abraham died and so did the prophets, yet you say that if anyone keeps your word, he'll never ever taste death. Surely you're not greater than our father Abraham? He died, and so did the prophets. So who on earth do you think you are?"

Jesus replied, "If I glorify myself, my glory means nothing. My Father, whom you claim as your God, is the one who glorifies me. Though you don't know him, I know him. If I said I didn't, I'd be a liar like you; but I do know him and keep his word. Your father Abraham was glad at the prospect of seeing my day; he saw it and rejoiced."

"You're not yet fifty years old," the Judeans responded, "and you've seen Abraham!"

"The truth is," Jesus answered, "that before Abraham existed, I am!"

At this, they picked up stones to stone him, but Jesus hid himself and left the temple.

Another holiday conflict

It was winter; the time for the *Feast of Dedication*[22] (*Feast of Lights*) came. Again Jesus was in the temple, walking about in Solomon's Colonnade. Some Judeans encircled him, saying, "How long will you keep us in suspense? If you're the Messiah, tell us plainly."

Jesus answered, "I did tell you, but you don't believe. The works I do in my Father's name testify for me; but you don't believe because you're not my sheep. My sheep heed my voice; I know them, and they follow me. I give them eternal life, so they'll never ever perish. No-one will snatch them out of my hand. My Father, who has given them to me, is greater than all; no-one is able to snatch them out of my Father's hand. I and the Father are one."

Again the Judeans picked up stones in order to stone him, but Jesus said to them, "I've shown you many great works from the Father; for which of these do you stone me?"

"We're not stoning you for any of these," replied the Judeans, "but for blasphemy, because you, a mere man, claim to be God."

Jesus answered them, "Isn't it written in your Law, 'I have said you're gods'? If he called them 'gods', to whom the word of God came – and the Scripture can't be broken – what about the one whom the Father set apart and sent into the world? Why do you accuse me of blasphemy because I said, 'I am God's Son'? Don't believe me unless I do what my Father does. But if I do it, even though you don't believe me, believe the miraculous works, so that you may know and understand that the Father is in me, and I am in the Father."

Again they tried to seize him, but he escaped from their grasp.

Man-made eyes?

Passing along, Jesus saw a man who had been blind from birth. His disciples asked him, "Rabbi, who sinned, this man or his parents, that he was born without eyes?"

"Neither this man nor his parents sinned," answered Jesus. "Rather ask, 'is there now an opportunity for the kingdom of God to be revealed in his life?' It's necessary, for as long as it's day, for us to do the work of the one who sent me. Night is coming, when no-one is able to work. While I'm in the world, I am the light of the world."

Having said this, he spat on the ground, made mud with the spittle, then filled the man's eye sockets with the mud! "Go," Jesus told him, "and wash in the Pool of Siloam" (this word means 'Sent'). So the man went and washed, and came back seeing.

His neighbours and those who had seen him formerly as a beggar asked, "Isn't this the same man who used to sit and beg?" Some claimed that it was he.

Others said, "No, but he does look like him."

However he kept insisting, "I am the man."

"So how were your eyes opened?" they demanded.

He replied, "The man they call Jesus made some mud and put it on my eyes. He told me to go to Siloam and wash. So I went and washed, and now I see."

"Where's this man?" they asked him.

"I don't know," he replied.

They took this once-sightless man to the Pharisees. Now the day, during which Jesus had made, with mud, the aperture for the man's eyes, was a Sabbath. So the Pharisees also asked him how he had received his sight. "He put mud on my eyes," the man replied, "I washed, and now I see."

Some of the Pharisees said, "That fellow isn't from God, he doesn't keep the Sabbath."

But others asked, "How can a man who's a sinner do such signs?" So there was a division of opinion amongst them.

Finally they turned again to the man who had been blind, "What have you to say about him, because it was your eyes he opened."

The man replied, "He's a prophet."

The religious Judeans still refused to believe that he had been blind and could now see, until they sent for the man's parents. They asked, "Is this your son, the one you say was born without eyes? How is it that he can see now?"

"We know he's our son," the parents answered, "and that he was born without eyes. But how he can see now, or who opened his eyes, we don't know. Ask him. He's old enough; he'll speak for himself."

His parents said this because they were afraid of the religious leaders, who had already decided that anyone who acknowledged that Jesus was the Messiah would be put out of the synagogue. That was why his parents said, "He's old enough; ask him."

So for the second time they called the man who had been blind. "Give glory to God," they said. "We know that this man is a sinner."

He replied, "Whether he's a sinner or not, I don't know. One thing I do know. I was blind but now I see!"

Then they asked him, "What did he do to you? How did he open your eyes?"

He answered, "I've told you already and you didn't listen. Why do you want to hear it again? Surely you don't want to become his disciples too?"

With that they threw insults at him and said, "You're this fellow's disciple! We're disciples of Moses! We know that God spoke to Moses, but as for this fellow, we don't even know where he comes from."

The man answered, "Now that's an amazing thing! You don't

know where he comes from, yet he opened my eyes. We know that God doesn't listen to sinners. He listens to the God-fearing man who does his will. Nobody has ever heard of opening the eyes of a man born blind like this. If this man weren't from God, he couldn't do anything."

To this they replied, "You were a total sinner at birth, yet you would teach us!"

So they excommunicated him.

Jesus heard that they had excommunicated the man. When he found him, he said, "Do you believe in the Son of Man?"

"Who is he, sir?" the man asked. "so that I may believe in him."

Jesus said, "You have now seen him; the one speaking with you is he."

Then the man said, "Lord, I believe," and he worshipped him.

Jesus said, "For judgment I've come into this world, so that the blind will see and those who see will become blind."

Some Pharisees who were with him heard him say this and asked, "What? Are we blind too?"

Jesus said, "If you were blind, you wouldn't be guilty of sin; but now that you claim you can see, your guilt remains."

Light in the darkness

Then Jesus began to speak to his disciples, saying: "Your eye is the lamp of your body. When your eyes are sound then your whole body also is full of light. But if your eyes are sick, your body also is full of darkness. If then the light within you is darkness, how great is that darkness! See to it, then, that the light within you isn't darkness. Therefore, if your whole body is full of light, with no part of it dark, it will be completely lit up, as when the light of a lamp shines on you."

Attending to Jesus

As Jesus and his disciples went on their way, they came to a village where a certain woman named Martha opened her home to them. She had a sister called Mary, who also went and sat at the Lord's feet listening to what he said. But Martha allowed her attention to wander because of all the preparations that had to be made. She came to him and asked, "Lord, don't you care that my sister has left me to serve by myself? Tell her to help me!"

"Martha, Martha," the Lord answered, "You're fretting and flustered about many things, but only one thing is needed. Mary has chosen what is better, and it won't be taken away from her."

Many believe

Then Jesus went back across the Jordan, into the region of Judea, to the place where, in the early days, John had been baptising. Here he stayed and many people came to him. They said, "John didn't do any miraculous signs, yet all that John said about this man was true."

Many people believed in him there.

CHAPTER 13

Terms of Endearment

Again large crowds of people came journeying along with Jesus. He healed them; and as was his custom, he kept teaching them.

Marriage and divorce

Some Pharisees came to test him by asking, "Is it lawful for a man to divorce his wife for any and every reason?"

"What did Moses command you?" he asked.

They said, "Moses permitted a man to write a certificate of divorce then send her away."

"It was because of your hard heartedness that Moses wrote you this commandment," Jesus replied. "But haven't you read, that from the beginning of creation God 'made them male and female' and 'For this reason a man will leave his father and mother and cleave permanently to his wife; the two becoming one flesh'? So they're no longer two, but one. Therefore what God has harnessed together, let no-one separate."

When they were in the house again, the disciples plied Jesus with questions about this issue. He answered, "Whoever divorces his wife and marries another woman commits adultery against her. If a wife divorces her husband and marries another man, she commits adultery; the man who marries a divorced woman commits adultery". I tell you that anyone who divorces his wife, except for marital infidelity, and marries another woman, causes her to commit adultery. Anyone who marries the divorced woman commits adultery."

The disciples said to him, "If that's the case, it's better not to marry."

Jesus replied, "Not everyone can accept this word, but only those to whom it's been given. Some men are eunuchs because they were born that way; others were made that way by men; others have renounced marriage for the sake of the kingdom of heaven. Let the one who can accept this receive it."

Jesus welcomes children

People were bringing babies and little children to Jesus for him to place his hands on them to bless them. When the disciples saw this, they sternly rebuked them, but without effect. When Jesus saw what they were doing, he was indignant. He said to them, "Let the little children come to me; stop hindering them, the kingdom of heaven belongs to such as these. I tell you truthfully, whoever doesn't receive the kingdom of God simply as child does, will never enter it."

So having taken them in his arms, he put his hands on them and blessed them warmly.

Then he went on from there.

Jesus sets priorities

As Jesus and the disciples were walking along the road, a teacher of the law came up to him and said, "Teacher, I will follow you wherever you go."

Jesus replied, "Foxes have holes and birds of the air have nests, but the Son of Man has nowhere to lay his head."

He said to another man, "Follow me."

But the man replied, "Lord, first let me go and bury my father."

"Let the dead bury their own dead", Jesus said, "but you go and proclaim the kingdom of God."

Yet another said, "I'll follow you, Lord; but first let me go back and say good-bye to my family."

Jesus replied, "No-one who puts their hand to the plough and then looks back is fit for the kingdom of God."

Serving

"Suppose one of you has a servant ploughing, or looking after the sheep. Would you say to the servant when he comes in from the field, 'Come along now and sit down to eat'? Wouldn't you rather say, 'Prepare my supper, make yourself ready and wait on me while I eat and drink; after that you can eat and drink'? Would you thank the servant because he did what he was told to do? So you also, when you've done everything you were told to do, should say, 'We're unworthy servants; we've only done our duty.'"

A lad in earnest

Now a certain ruler ran towards Jesus and knelt before him asking, "Good Teacher, what good thing must I do in order to inherit eternal life?"

"Why do you say that I'm good and ask me about good things?" Jesus answered. "No-one is good – except one – God. If you want to enter LIFE, you know the commandments, obey them."

"Which ones?" the man inquired.

Jesus replied, "Don't murder; don't commit adultery; don't steal; don't give false testimony; don't defraud; honour your father and mother,' and 'love your neighbour as yourself.'"

"Teacher," the young man declared, "all these I've taken care not to violate since I was a boy. What am I still lacking?"

When he heard this, Jesus gazed at him and LOVED him. He said to him, "You still lack one thing. If you want to complete the set, go at once, sell everything you possess and give to the poor so you'll have treasure in heaven. Then come and begin following me."

When the young man heard this he was crestfallen and he went away sad, because he had great wealth.

Then Jesus, having glanced swiftly around, said to his disciples, "Truthfully, it's hard for those who keep holding on to wealth to enter the kingdom of heaven. I tell you, it's easier for a cable to go through the eye of a needle than for a rich man to enter the kingdom of God."

When the disciples heard this, they were utterly amazed at his words, saying to one another, "Who then can be saved?"

Jesus looked at them and said, "With human power this is impossible, but all things are possible in the presence of God."

Peter said, "Look, we've abandoned everything to follow you! What's in it for us?"

Jesus replied, "Truthfully, no-one, who's abandoned home or brothers or sisters or mother or father or children or fields for me and the good news, will fail to receive a hundred times as much in this present age (homes, brothers, sisters, mothers, children and fields) – with persecutions. And in the age to come, they will inherit eternal life. I tell you the truth, at the renewal of all things, when the Son of Man sits on his glorious throne, you who've followed me will also sit on twelve thrones, judging the twelve tribes of Israel. But many who are first will be last and many who are last will be first."

Equality in the kingdom

"You see," continued Jesus, "the kingdom of heaven is like a landowner who went out early in the morning to hire men to work in his vineyard. He agreed to pay them a fixed rate for the day and sent them to his vineyard.

About nine o'clock he went and saw others standing idle in the marketplace. He said to these, 'You also go and work in my vineyard, and I'll pay you whatever I consider right.' So they went.

He went out again at about noon and at three o'clock and did the same thing. At about five o'clock, he went out and still found others standing around. He asked them, 'Why have you been standing here all day long doing nothing?' 'Because no-one hired us,' they answered.

He said to them, 'You also go and work in my vineyard.'

When evening came (at six o'clock), the vineyard owner said to his foreman, 'Call the workers and pay them their wages, beginning with the last ones I hired, then going on to the first.'

The workers who were hired about five o'clock came and each received the full daily rate. So when those who were hired first came, they expected to receive a larger sum. But each one of them also received the daily rate. When they received it, they began to grumble against the landowner. 'These men you hired last worked only one hour,' they said, 'and you've made them equal to us who've borne the burden of the work, and the scorching heat.'

But he answered one of them, 'Friend, I'm not cheating you. Didn't you make an agreement with me for a fixed sum? Take your pay and go. I choose to give the man who was hired last the same as I gave you. Aren't I allowed to do what I want with my own things? Or are you begrudging because I'm benevolent?'

So this is what I meant when I said the last will be first, and the first will be last."

Seventy sent too

After this the Lord appointed seventy others and sent them out two-by-two ahead of him to every town and place where he was about to go. *He instructed them as he had The Twelve saying,* "Don't greet anyone on the road. When you enter a house, first say, 'Peace to this house.' If a man of peace is there, your peace will rest on him; if not, it will return to you. Stay in that house, eating and drinking whatever they give you, for the worker is worthy of his wages. Don't move around from house to house. When you enter a town and are welcomed, heal the sick that are there and tell them, 'The kingdom of God has come near to you.' But when you enter a town and aren't welcomed, go into its streets and say, 'Even the dust of your town that sticks to our feet we wipe off against you. Yet be sure of this: The kingdom of God is near.'

Whoever listens to you listens to me; whoever rejects you rejects me; and whoever rejects me rejects him who sent me."

Reasons for rejoicing

Later… The seventy returned with joy, saying, "Lord, even the demons submit to us in your name."

He replied, "I was seeing Satan fall like lightning from heaven. Look, I've given you authority to trample on snakes and scorpions and to overcome all the power of the enemy; nothing will harm you. However, don't rejoice just because the spirits submit to you; rather rejoice that your names are recorded in heaven."

At that same time Jesus, full of the Holy Spirit, rejoiced exuberantly, saying, "I praise you, Father, Lord of heaven and earth, though you've concealed these things from the wise and clever, you've revealed them to simple folk. Yes, Father, this delights you.

All things have been handed to me by my Father. No-one knows who the Son is except the Father, and no-one knows who the Father is, except the Son and anyone to whom the Son chooses to reveal him.

Come to me, all you who are weary and burdened and I'll give you relief. Take my yoke upon you and learn from me, for I'm gentle and humble in heart. You'll find relief for your souls; for my yoke is easy and my burden is light."

Then he turned to his disciples and said privately, "Blessed are the eyes that see what you see. I tell you that many prophets and kings wanted to see what you see but didn't see it, and to hear what you hear but didn't hear it."

Neighbours

On one occasion a lawyer stood up to test Jesus. "Teacher," he asked, "what should I have done to inherit eternal life?"

"What's written in the Law?" Jesus replied. "How do you read it?"

The lawyer answered, "You must LOVE the Lord your God from all your heart, with all your soul, with all your strength and with all your mind' and, 'Love your neighbour as yourself.'"

"You've answered correctly," Jesus replied. "Keep doing this and you'll live."

But wanting to justify himself, he asked Jesus, "And who's my neighbour?"

In response Jesus said, "Once upon a time, a man was going down from Jerusalem to Jericho when he was attacked by bandits. They stripped him, beat him and fled, leaving him half dead. By chance a priest happened to be going down that road but when he saw the man, he passed by on the other side! So too, a Levite: when he came to the place and saw the man, he also passed by on the other side! But a Samaritan also was travelling along the road, when he came across the man, he had compassion for him. He approached the man, bandaged his wounds, pouring on oil and wine. Then, after putting the man on his own beast, he brought him to an inn and cared for him. The next day he took out two silver coins and gave them to the innkeeper. 'Look after him,' he said, 'and when I return, I'll reimburse you for any additional expense you may have had.'

Which of these three do you think was a neighbour to the man who was mugged?"

The lawyer replied, "The one who had mercy on him."

Jesus told him, "Go, and you keep doing the same."

A prayer template (commonly called 'The Lord's Prayer')

One day Jesus was praying in a certain place; as he was finishing, one of his disciples said to him, "Lord, teach us to pray, just as John taught his disciples."

He said to them, "This is the pattern for your prayers and what you may say:

'Our Dear Father in heaven

    let your name be held in reverence,

        let your kingdom come,

            let your will be done on earth as it is done in heaven.

Give us each day our daily bread.

Forgive us our sins, as we forgive those indebted to us.

And lead us not into temptation but deliver us from the evil one.'"

Asking

Then he said to them, "Which of you has a friend to whom you could go at midnight and say, 'Friend, lend me three loaves of bread, because a friend of mine has arrived after a journey and I've nothing to set before him'?

Then suppose the one inside answers, 'Don't bother me. The door's already locked, and my children and I are in bed. I can't get up and give you anything.' I tell you, though he won't get up and give you the bread because he's your friend, yet because of your bold persistence he'll get up and give you as much as you need.

So I say to you: keep on asking and it will be given to you; keep on seeking and you'll find; keep on knocking and the door will be opened to you. For everyone who asks receives; he who seeks finds; and to him who knocks, the door will be opened.

Which of you fathers, if your son asks for bread, will give him a stone, if he asks for a fish, will give him a snake instead? Or if he asks for an egg, will give him a scorpion? If you then, though you're evil, know how to give good gifts to your children, how much more will your Father in heaven give good gifts *and* the Holy Spirit to those who ask him?

Again, I tell you that if two of you on earth agree about anything you ask for, it will be done for you by my Father in heaven. For where two or three come together in my name, I'm right there with them."

Persistence in prayer

Then, to show them that they should always pray and not lose heart, Jesus told his disciples a parable. He said: "In a certain town there was a judge who neither feared God nor respected people. Now there was a widow in that town who kept coming to him saying, 'Grant me justice against my opponent.'

For some time he was unwilling to do so. But finally he said to himself, 'Even though I neither fear God nor respect people, because this widow keeps pestering me, I'll see that she receives justice, so that she won't wear me out eventually with her coming!'"

The Lord said, "Listen to what the unjust judge says. Will not God bring about justice for his chosen ones, with whom he has patience, when they cry out to him day and night? I tell you, he will see that they receive justice – speedily. Yet, when the Son of Man comes, will he find faith on the earth?"

Pride in prayer

Jesus told this parable to those who were confident of their own righteousness but despised everyone else: "Two men went up to the temple to pray, one was a Pharisee and the other a tax collector. The Pharisee, standing by himself, prayed: 'God, I thank you that I'm not like other people – robbers, rogues, adulterers – or even like this tax collector. I fast twice a week and give a tenth of all I receive.'

But the tax collector stood at a distance. He wouldn't even look up to heaven, but beat his breast and said, 'God, have mercy on me, the sinner.'

I tell you that this man, rather than the other, went home justified before God.

For those who exalt themselves will be humbled, and those who humble themselves will be exalted."

Obey the word of God

As Jesus was saying these things, a woman in the crowd called out, "Blessed is the womb that carried you, and the breasts you sucked."

He replied, "On the contrary, blessed rather are those who hear the word of God and obey it."

CHAPTER 14

Challenging Followers

Possessions

Once when a crowd of many thousands had gathered, such that they were trampling on one another, someone in the crowd said to him, "Teacher, tell my brother to divide our inheritance with me."

Jesus replied, "Man, who appointed me a judge or an arbitrator between you?" Then he said to them, "Watch out! Be on your guard against the consuming drive to acquire things. For people's lives don't consist in the abundance of their possessions."

And he told them this parable: "The farm of a certain rich man was prolifically productive. So he reasoned with himself, 'What shall I do? I've no space to store my crops. I know, this is what I'll do. I'll tear down my barns and build bigger ones. There I'll store all my grain and my goods.' Then he said to himself, 'You've plenty of goods stored up for many years. Take it easy; eat, drink and be merry.'

But God said to him, 'You foolish man! During this very night your life will be demanded from you. Then who'll inherit what you've prepared for yourself?'

This is how it will be with anyone who stores up things for themselves, but isn't rich towards God."

Don't Worry

Then Jesus said to his disciples: "I'm telling you, don't be anxious about your life, what you'll eat; nor about your body, what you'll wear. Life is more important than food; the body more important than clothes. Consider the birds, the ravens for example: they neither sow nor reap, they've neither storerooms nor barns; yet God, your heavenly Father, feeds them. How much more valuable you are than birds! Who of you, by worrying, can add a single hour to his lifespan? Since you can't do this very little thing, why do you worry about the rest?

Consider how the lilies of the field grow. They neither toil nor spin. Yet I tell you, not even Solomon in his entire splendour clothed himself like one of these. If that's how God clothes the grass of the field, which is here today, and tomorrow is thrown into an oven, how much more will he clothe you? O you of little faith! So don't fret, saying 'What shall we eat?' or 'What shall we drink?' or 'What shall we wear?' The people of the world strive after all these things, but your heavenly Father knows that you need them. Therefore seek first his kingdom and his righteousness, and these things will be given to you as well. Don't worry about tomorrow, for tomorrow will worry about itself. Each day has enough trouble of its own.

Don't be afraid, little flock; it's your Father's delight to give you the kingdom. Sell your possessions and keep giving generously to those in need. By doing this you will be providing purses for yourselves that won't wear out; an inexhaustible treasure in heaven, where no thief disturbs and no moth destroys. For where your treasure is, there your heart will be also."

Repent or perish

At that time, some people came and reported to Jesus about the Galileans whose blood Pilate had mingled with their sacrificial offerings. Jesus responded, "Do you think that these Galileans were worse sinners than other Galileans because they suffered this way? No, but I tell you, unless you repent, you too will all perish. Or those eighteen who were killed when the tower in Siloam fell on them – do you think they were greater sinners than others living in Jerusalem? I tell you, no! But unless you repent, you too will all perish."

A reprieved fig tree

Then he told this parable: "A certain man had a fig tree which he'd planted in his vineyard. He went looking for fruit on it, but didn't find any. So he said to the vinedresser, 'For the past three years I've been coming looking for fruit on this fig tree and haven't found any. Cut it down! Why should it use up the soil?'

"'Sir,' the vinedresser replied, 'leave it alone this year; I'll dig around it and manure it, and if it fruits next year, fine! If not, then cut it down.'"

A reprieved cripple

One Sabbath Jesus was teaching in one of the synagogues. A woman was there who'd had a crippling spirit for eighteen years. She was bent over and could not stand up straight at all. When Jesus saw her, he called her forward and said to her, "Woman, you're set free from your infirmity." He put his hands on her, and straightaway she straightened up and praised God.

Being indignant because Jesus had healed on the Sabbath, the synagogue ruler said to the crowd, "There are six days for work. So come and be healed on those days, not on the Sabbath."

The Lord answered him, "You hypocrites! Doesn't each of you on the Sabbath loose his ox or ass from its stall and lead it out to drink? Then shouldn't this daughter of Abraham, whom Satan has kept bound these past eighteen years, be loosed on the Sabbath day from her bondage?"

When he said this, all his opponents were put to shame, but the people were delighted with all the glorious things being accomplished by him.

No reprieve for religious leaders

When Jesus had finished speaking, a Pharisee invited him to have a mid-day meal with him; so having gone into the house he reclined at the table. The Pharisee was amazed when he saw that Jesus did not first ritually wash before the meal.

But the Lord said to him, "You Pharisees clean the outside of the cup and dish, but inside you're full of greed, self-indulgence and wickedness. You foolish, blind people! Didn't the one who made the outside make the inside also? First clean the inside of the cup and dish, then the outside will be clean as well. In fact, give what's inside the dish to the poor, then everything will be clean for you.

Woe betide you Pharisees, because you give God a tenth of your mint, rue, dill, cumin and all other kinds of garden herbs – and your spices, but you neglect the more important matters of the law – justice, mercy, faithfulness and the love of God. You should've practised the latter without leaving the former undone. You blind guides; you filter your wine to strain out a gnat but swallow a camel!

Woe betide you Pharisees, because you love the place of honour in the synagogues, and being greeted in the marketplaces.

Woe betide you, for you're like unmarked graves which people walk over without knowing it."

One of the lawyers answered him, "Teacher, in saying these things, you insult us also."

Jesus replied, "Yes, woe betide you lawyers also, because you burden people with loads that are difficult to carry, yet you yourselves won't lift one finger to help them.

Woe betide you, because you decorate the monuments of the

righteous and build memorials to the prophets; yet it was your forefathers who killed them. You say, 'If we'd lived in the days of our forefathers we wouldn't have taken part with them in the shedding of their blood'. But you testify that you're in agreement with what your forefathers did; they killed the prophets and now you build their monuments.

You can fill up then the measure of their sin because I, the Wisdom of God, will send you prophets and apostles, wise men and teachers, some of whom you'll kill and crucify, others you'll flog in your synagogues and persecute in your towns. Therefore this generation will be held responsible for the righteous blood of all the prophets that's been shed since the beginning of the world – from the blood of innocent Abel to the blood of Zechariah son of Berekiah, who was killed between the temple and the altar. Yes, I tell you, this generation will be held responsible for it all.

Woe betide you lawyers, you hypocrites, you've taken away the key to knowledge. You shut the kingdom of heaven in people's faces. You yourselves haven't entered, and you have hindered those who are trying to enter."

When Jesus left there, the Pharisees and the teachers of the law began to be very hostile. They besieged him with questions, plotting to catch him out in something he might say.

Another Sabbath set-up

Another Sabbath, when Jesus went to a meal at the house of a prominent Pharisee, he was being closely watched. And there in front of him was a man suffering from dropsy. Jesus asked the Pharisees and the lawyers, "Is it permissible to heal on the Sabbath, or not?" But they remained silent; so taking hold of the man, he healed him and sent him away.

Then he asked them, "If one of you has a son, or even an ox, that falls into a well on the Sabbath day, won't you immediately pull him out?" But they stayed silent, having nothing to say against these things.

Pride of place

Noticing how the guests picked the places of privilege at the table, he told them this parable: "When someone invites you to a wedding reception, don't take the place of honour, because a person more honourable than you may have been invited. Then the host will come and say to you 'Give this person your place.' Humiliated, you'll have to take the least important place. But when you're invited, take the lowest place, so that when your host comes, he'll say to you, 'Friend, move up higher.' Then you'll be honoured in the presence of all your fellow guests. You see, all who exalt themselves will be humbled, but all who humble themselves will be exalted."

Holy hospitality

Then Jesus said to the man who'd invited him, "When you hold a lunch or dinner party, don't make a practice of inviting only your friends, your brothers or relatives, or your rich neighbours – who'll repay you by inviting you back. But when you prepare a party, invite the poor, the crippled, the lame and the blind – they don't have the means to repay you – and you'll be blessed. Indeed you'll be rewarded at the resurrection of the righteous."

When one of those at the table with Jesus heard this, self-satisfied, he said, "Blessed is the one who's invited to eat at the feast in the kingdom of God."

Jesus responded: "A certain man was holding a sumptuous supper party for many invited guests. When the day of the meal came he sent his servant to tell those who'd been invited, 'Come, for everything is now ready.'

But all alike they began to make excuses: The first said to him, 'I've just bought a field, it's imperative that I go and inspect it. Please have me excused.' Another said, 'I've just bought five yoke of oxen, I'm on my way to test-drive them. Please excuse me.' Still another said, 'I've just been married, therefore I can't come.'

So the servant returned and reported this to his master. Then the owner of the house became angry and said to his servant, 'Quickly, go out into the town squares and streets and bring in the poor, the crippled, the blind and the lame.'

'Sir,' the servant said, 'what you ordered has been done, but still there are places'.

Then the master told his servant, 'Go out further to the highways and hedges and urge them to come in, so that my house will be full. I tell you, none of those who were originally invited will have a taste of my supper.'"

Counting the cost

Large crowds were travelling with Jesus. Turning to them he said: "If anyone comes to me and doesn't hate his father and mother, his spouse, his children and his siblings – yes, even his own life – he can't be my disciple. Anyone who doesn't carry his cross and follow me can't be my disciple.

Which one of you who, wanting to build a tower, won't first sit down and count the cost to see if you have enough cash to complete it? If you lay the foundation but aren't able to finish it, everyone who sees it will ridicule you, saying, 'This person began to build but wasn't able to finish.'

Or what king, who's about to engage another king in battle, won't first sit down and consider whether, with ten thousand men, he's able to face the one coming against him with twenty thousand?

Otherwise, while the other is still a long way off, he'll send an ambassador to ask for terms of peace.

In the same way, if any of you doesn't renounce all your possessions you can't be my disciple.

"Now think carefully about what you've heard."

CHAPTER 15

Love's Labours

Tax-collectors, and others considered to be social misfits, were all gathering around to hear what Jesus had to say. But the Pharisees and the teachers of the law kept grumbling, "This fellow welcomes sinners and even eats with them."

The lost sheep

So Jesus told them this parable: "Which man having a hundred sheep and losing one of them, wouldn't leave the ninety-nine in the open pastures and go after the lost one until he finds it? When he finds it, he'd joyfully put it on his shoulders and go home. Then he'd call his friends and neighbours together saying, 'Celebrate with me; I've found my lost sheep.' I tell you that in the same way there'll be more rejoicing in heaven over one sinner who repents than over ninety-nine righteous persons who think they have no need to repent.

The lost silver

"Or what woman having ten silver coins and losing one, doesn't light a lamp, sweep the house and search carefully until she finds it? When she finds it, she calls her friends and neighbours together saying, 'Rejoice with me; I've found my lost coin.' In the same way, I tell you, there's jubilation in the presence of the angels of God over every single sinner who repents."

The lost son

Jesus continued saying, "Once there was a man who had two sons. The younger one said to his father, 'Father, give me the share of the property that's coming to me.' So the father apportioned his property between them.

A few days later, the younger son gathered together everything he had and travelled to a faraway country. There he wasted his wealth on a prodigal lifestyle. After he'd spent the lot, there was a severe famine throughout that country so he began to be in need. Therefore he went and hitched himself to one of the citizens, who sent him into his fields to feed pigs. He would gladly have gorged himself on the pods which the pigs were eating, but no-one gave him anything.

This brought him to his senses and he said to himself, 'How many of my father's hired servants have more bread than they can eat, while I'm here dying of starvation? I'll get up and go back to my father and I'll say to him: Father, I've sinned against heaven and in your sight. I don't deserve to be called your son; make me like one of your hired servants.' So he got up and returned to his father.

But, while the lad was still some distance away, his father saw him. Filled with compassion, at full pelt, he ran to his son, threw his arms around his neck and smothered him with kisses.

The son said to him, 'Father, I've sinned against heaven and in your sight. I'm no longer worthy to be called your son.'

However the father said to his servants, 'Swiftly now! Bring the finest robe and put it on him. Put the family insignia ring on his finger and the bespoke shoes on his feet. Bring the fattened calf and kill it. Let's celebrate and be merry because this son of mine was dead and is alive again; he had been lost and is now found.' So they began to celebrate.

Meanwhile the elder son was returning home from the fields. When he came near the house, he heard music and dancing. So he summoned one of the servants and asked him what was going on. 'Your brother's here,' he replied, 'and your father has killed the fattened calf, because he's received his son back, safe and sound.'

The elder son became angry and refused to go in, so his father came out and pleaded with him. But he remonstrated with his father saying, 'Look! All these years I've slaved for you, never disobeying your orders. Yet you never gave me even a young goat so I could celebrate with my friends. But when this son of yours, who's squandered your wealth on prostitutes, comes home, you sacrifice the fattened calf for him!'

'My dear son,' the father said, 'you're always with me, and everything I have is yours. But it's only right that we celebrate and be glad, because this is your brother who was dead but is now alive; he was lost but now is found.'"

The lost job

Jesus then told his disciples: "There was a certain rich man who had a manager who was accused of squandering his master's possessions. So the rich man called him in and asked him, 'What's this I hear about you? Give me the record books, because you can't be manager any longer.'

The manager said to himself, 'What shall I do now? My boss is taking away my job. I'm not strong enough to dig, and I'm ashamed to beg – I know what I'll do so that, when I lose my job here, people will welcome me into their houses.'

So he summoned each one of his boss's debtors. He asked the first, 'How much do you owe my boss?' 'Eight hundred gallons of olive oil,' he replied.

The manager told him, 'Quickly take your bill, make it four hundred and pay now.'

Then he asked the second, 'How much do you owe?' 'A thousand bushels of wheat,' he replied. He told him, 'Take your bill, make it eight hundred and pay now.'

The rich man commended the dishonest manager because he'd acted shrewdly.

For the people of this age are shrewder in dealing with their peers than the people of light. I tell you, use unrighteous wealth to gain friends for yourselves, so that when it fails, you'll be welcomed into eternal dwellings.

The one who is faithful with little is faithful with much, and one who's dishonest with very little will also be dishonest with much. So if you haven't been faithful in handling unrighteous wealth, who will entrust you with true riches? And if you haven't been faithful with someone else's things, who will give you your own things?"

The Pharisees, who loved money, heard all these things and ridiculed Jesus. He said to them, "You're the ones who justify yourselves in the eyes of men, but God knows your hearts. What is highly esteemed among men is an abomination in God's sight."

The lost soul

Continuing, Jesus said, "There was a rich man who dressed in purple and fine clothes. Every day he ate sumptuously, passing his time in splendid ease. A beggar named Lazarus who had been placed at his gate longed to feed from what fell from the rich man's table. Lazarus was covered with ulcers, which even the dogs came and licked.

In the course of time the poor man died and the angels carried him away to Abraham's side. The rich man also died and was buried. In hell, where he was in torment, he looked up. From far away, he saw Abraham with Lazarus at his side. So he called to him, 'Father

Abraham, have mercy on me and send Lazarus to dip the tip of his finger in water and cool my tongue, because I'm suffering agony in these flames.'

But Abraham replied, 'Son, remember that in your lifetime you received your good things, while Lazarus received bad things; but now he's comforted here and you are suffering. Besides all this, between us and you a great chasm has been fixed; so that those wanting to go from here to you can't. Neither can anyone cross over from where you are to us.'

He answered, 'Then I ask you, Father, send Lazarus to my father's house, for I've five brothers. Let him warn them, so that they also won't come to this place of torment.'

Abraham replied, 'They have Moses and the Prophets; let your brothers listen to them.'

'No, no, Father Abraham,' he said, 'but if someone from the dead goes to them, they'll repent.'

He said to him, 'If they don't listen to Moses and the Prophets, they won't be persuaded even if someone should rise from the dead.'"

Destiny calls

As the time was approaching for Jesus eventually to be taken up to heaven, he resolutely set his face to go to Jerusalem. He took The Twelve aside privately and began speaking about the things which were about to converge, saying, "We're going up to Jerusalem, and everything that's written about the Son of Man, by the prophets, will be fulfilled. He'll be betrayed to the chief priests and the teachers of the law who will condemn him to death. He will be handed over to the Romans. They'll mock him, mistreat him, insult him and spit on him. And, having whipped him, he'll be crucified. On the third day he will be raised back to life!"

The disciples did not understand any of this. Its meaning was hidden from them, so they didn't grasp what he was talking about.

Jesus sent messengers on ahead, who went into a Samaritan village to make things ready for him; but the people there did not welcome him, because his purpose was to travel to Jerusalem. When the disciples James and John saw this, they asked, "Lord, do you want us to call fire down from heaven, to consume them?" But Jesus turned and rebuked them saying, "You don't have the right spirit; the Son of Man hasn't come to destroy lives but to save them." So they went to another village.

Then the mother of Zebedee's sons came with them to Jesus and, kneeling down, asked a favour of him.

"What do you want me to do for you?" he asked.

She said, "Grant that these two sons of mine may sit one at your right and the other at your left, in your kingdom glory."

"You don't know what you are asking for yourselves," Jesus said to them. "Can you drink the cup I'm going to drink or be baptised with the baptism with which I'm baptised?"

"We can," they answered.

Jesus said to them, "You will indeed drink from my cup and be baptised with the baptism I'm baptised with, but to sit at my right or left is not for me to grant. These places belong to those for whom they've been prepared by my Father."

The Life giver

When the ten heard about this, they were filled with indignation towards James and John. So Jesus called them together and said, "You know that those who are esteemed as rulers of the nations subjugate the people and their high officials are domineering. But that's not to be so with you. Instead, whoever wants to become great among you must be your servant; whoever desires to be first must be the slave of all. Even the Son of Man didn't come to be served, but to serve, and to give his life to pay the ransom for many."

CHAPTER 16

On the Way

They were now on the road, going up to Jerusalem, with Jesus, as usual, leading the way. The disciples were astonished by his majestic bearing, while those who followed along were afraid.

The thankful man

While on the way to Jerusalem, Jesus travelled along the border between Samaria and Galilee. He went into a particular village where ten men, who had leprosy, approached him. They stood at a distance and called out in a loud voice, "Jesus, Master, have pity on us!"

Having seen them, he responded, "Go and show yourselves to the priests." As they went, they were cured.

One of them, realising that he was healed, came back, praising God in a loud voice. He threw himself on his face at Jesus' feet and thanked him – he was a Samaritan.

Jesus asked, "Weren't there ten who were cured? Where are the other nine? Was no-one found to return and give praise to God except this foreigner?" Then Jesus said to him, "Rise and go; your faith has made you whole."

Salvation – The narrow door

Then Jesus went on through the towns and villages, teaching, as he journeyed towards Jerusalem. Someone asked him, "Lord, are only a few people going to be saved?"

He said to them, "Strive eagerly to enter through the narrow door. I tell you, many will try to enter but won't be able to because once the owner of the house rises and shuts the door, you'll stand outside knocking and pleading, 'Sir, open up for us.'

He'll answer, 'I don't know you. Where do you come from?'

Then you'll begin to say, 'We ate and drank with you, and you taught in our streets.'

But he'll repeat, 'I tell you, I don't know you nor where you've come from. Go away from me, all you evil-doers!'

There'll be weeping and gnashing of teeth when you see Abraham, Isaac and Jacob and all the prophets in the kingdom of God, but you yourselves are thrown out. People will come from the east and west, the north and south, and will recline at the banquet table in the kingdom of God. Indeed there are those who are last who'll be first, and first who'll be last."

Salvation – the gate

"I tell you the truth, the one who doesn't enter the sheep pen by the gate, but climbs in by some other way, is a sneak thief and a bandit. The one who enters by the gate is the shepherd of the sheep. The gatekeeper opens the gate for him, and the sheep listen to his voice. He calls his own sheep by name and leads them out. When he has brought out all his own, he goes on ahead of them, his sheep follow him because they know his voice. But they'll never follow a stranger; they'll run away from him because they don't recognise a stranger's voice." Jesus used this allegory, but they did not understand what he was telling them.

So Jesus said again, "I tell you the truth, I am the gate for the sheep. All who ever came before me were thieves and bandits, but the sheep didn't listen to them. I am the gate; whoever enters through me will be saved. He'll go in and out, and find pasture. The thief comes only to steal and to kill and to destroy; I've come that they may have life, and have it beyond measure."

Salvation – the shepherd

"I am the good shepherd. The good shepherd – the beautiful one – lays down his life for the sheep. The hired hand isn't the shepherd who owns the sheep. So when the hired hand sees the wolf coming, he leaves the sheep and runs away, allowing the wolf to snatch the sheep and scatter the flock. The man runs away because he's a hired hand, caring nothing for the sheep.

I am the good shepherd; I know my own sheep and my own sheep know me – just as the Father knows me and I know the Father – and I lay down my life for the sheep. I have other sheep who aren't of this sheep-fold. I must bring them too. They'll recognise my voice, and so there'll be one flock and one Shepherd. The Father LOVES me because I lay down my life – that I can take it up again. No-one takes it from me, but I lay it down of my own will. I've authority to lay it down and I've authority to take it up again. These instructions I've received from my Father."

Because of these words the Judeans were again divided. Many of them were saying, 'He's demon-possessed and raving mad. Why do you listen to him?' But others were saying, 'These aren't the sayings of a man possessed by a demon. Surely a demon can't open the eyes of the blind?'

Having been asked by the Pharisees when the kingdom of God would come, Jesus answered, "The kingdom of God doesn't only come with things you can observe, nor will people be able to say, 'Look, here it is,' or 'There it is,' because the kingdom of God is here amongst you."

Days of salvation

Then he said to his disciples, "The time will come when you'll long to see one of the days of the Son of Man, but you'll not see it. People will tell you, 'There he is!' or 'Here he is!' Don't go after them nor pursue them. Just as the lightning flashes and lights up the sky from one end to the other so will be the Son of Man in his day. But first it's necessary for him to endure much suffering and be rejected by this generation.

Just as it was in the days of Noah, so it will be in the days of the Son of Man. In the days before the flood people were eating, drinking, marrying and being given in marriage, right up to the day Noah entered the ark. They didn't understand what hit them until the flood came and took them all away, and destroyed them."

Day of revelation

"It was the same in the days of Lot. People were eating and drinking, buying and selling, planting and building. But on the day Lot left Sodom, fire and sulphur rained down from heaven, destroying everything.

It'll be exactly like that on the day the Son of Man is revealed. On that day no-one on the roof of his house, with his belongings inside, should go down to save them. Likewise, no one in a field should return for anything. Remember Lot's wife! I tell you, on that night two people will be in one bed; one will be taken and the other will be left. Two women will be grinding grain together with a hand mill; one will be taken and the other will be left. Two men will be in the field; one will be taken and the other will be left."

"Where, Lord?" they asked.

He replied, "Where there's a corpse, there the vultures will gather."

Salvation for Lazarus

It happened that a man named Lazarus was ill. He was from Bethany, the village where Mary and her sister Martha lived. Lazarus was their brother. So the sisters sent for Jesus saying, "Lord, the one you're fond of is seriously sick."

When he heard this message, Jesus said, "This sickness won't end in death. No, it's for God's glory so that God's Son may be glorified through it." Jesus loved Martha, her sister and Lazarus; yet when he heard that Lazarus was sick, he remained where he was for two more days.

Then he said to his disciples, "Let's go into Judea again."

"But Rabbi," they said, "just recently the Judeans were trying to stone you, yet you're going back there?"

Jesus answered, "Aren't there twelve hours of daylight? Those who walk by day won't stumble, for they see by this world's light. It's when they walk by night that they stumble, because they have no light."

After he had said this, he went on to say to them, "Our friend Lazarus has fallen asleep; but I'm going to waken him."

His disciples therefore replied, "Lord, if he's fallen asleep, he'll get better." However Jesus had been speaking of his death, but the men thought he meant asleep, resting.

So Jesus spoke plainly to them, "Lazarus is dead, and for your sake I'm glad I wasn't there, so that you may believe. Let's go to him."

Then Thomas said to the rest of the disciples, "Let's go too, we may as well die with him!"

When Jesus arrived, he found that Lazarus had been in the tomb for four days already. Bethany was only about two miles from Jerusalem so a considerable number of Judeans had come to Martha and Mary to console them because of the loss of their brother. When Martha heard that Jesus had come, she went out to meet him, but Mary stayed seated in the house.

"Lord," Martha said to Jesus, "if only you'd been here, this brother of mine wouldn't have died. Yet even now I know that whatever you ask from God, God will give you."

Jesus said to her, "Your brother will rise again."

"I know he'll rise again in the resurrection on the last day," Martha replied.

Jesus said to her, "I am the resurrection and the LIFE. Whoever believes in me will live, even though he dies; and whoever lives and believes in me will never, ever die. Do you believe this?"

"Yes, Lord," she told him, "I believe that you're the Messiah, the Son of God, the one whom the world has been waiting for."

Having said this, she went back and called her sister Mary. Discreetly she said, "The Teacher is here. He is asking for you." When Mary heard this, she rose up quickly and went to him. Now Jesus had not yet entered the village, but was still at the place where Martha had met him. When the Judeans who'd been with Mary in the house, commiserating with her, noticed how quickly she arose and left, they followed her, supposing she was going to the tomb to mourn there.

When Mary reached the place where Jesus was and saw him, she fell at his feet saying, "Lord, if only you'd been here, my dear brother wouldn't have died."

When Jesus saw her weeping, and the Judeans who'd come with her weeping also, he gave way to his distress of spirit so that his body trembled. "Where have you put him?" he asked.

"Come and see, Lord," they replied.

Jesus wept.

Then the Judeans said, "See how he loved him!"

But some of them said, "Couldn't he, who opened the eyes of the blind man, have kept this man from dying?"

Jesus, once more being deeply moved, came to the tomb. It was a cave with a stone lying across its entrance. "Take away the stone," he said.

"But, Lord," Martha protested, "by this time there's a stench – he's been there four days."

Then Jesus said to her, "Didn't I tell you that if you believe, you'd see the glory of God?"

So they lifted away the stone. Jesus raised his eyes and said, "Father, I thank you that you've heard me. I know that you always hear me, but I say this because of the people standing here, that they may believe that you sent me."

Having said this, Jesus cried out in a loud voice, "Lazarus, come out!" The man who had died came out, his hands and feet bound with grave cloths, and a cloth around his face.

Jesus said to them, "Untie him and let him go."

Faith, phobias and plots

Having seen what Jesus did, many of the Judeans who'd come to visit Mary, put their faith in him. But some of them went to the Pharisees and told them what Jesus had done.

So the chief priests and the Pharisees convened the Sanhedrin.

"What are we doing?" they asked. "Here's this man performing many miraculous signs. If we let him go on like this, everyone will believe in him. This will result in the Romans coming and taking away both our holy place and our nation itself."

Then one of them, named Caiaphas, who was high priest that year, spoke up, "You know nothing at all! Don't you reckon that it's expedient that one man dies on behalf of the people, rather than the whole nation be destroyed?"

(He did not say this by his own reasoning, but as high priest that year he prophesied that Jesus was about to die on behalf of the nation; not for that nation only but also on behalf of the scattered children of God, to bring them together and make them one.)

So from that day on they plotted to kill him.

About that time some Pharisees came to Jesus and said to him, "Get away from here and go somewhere else. Herod wants to kill you."

He replied, "Go and say to that fox, 'I'll drive out demons and heal people today and tomorrow, and on the third day I'll reach my goal.' In any case, I must keep going today and tomorrow and the next day – for surely no prophet can die outside Jerusalem!

"O Jerusalem, Jerusalem, the city that kills the prophets and stones those sent to it, how often I've longed to gather your children together, as a hen gathers her chicks under her wings, but you wouldn't have it! Look, your house is left unprotected, forsaken by God. I tell you, you won't see me again until you say, 'Blessed is he who comes in the name of the Lord.'"

So Jesus no longer moved about openly among the Judeans. Instead he went to a region near the wilderness, to a village called Ephraim, where he stayed with his disciples.

Salvation for Zacchaeus

Then they went to Jericho. Jesus entered the city and was passing through. A man was there, named Zacchaeus, who was a chief tax collector – he was very wealthy. He had been wanting to see Jesus, to find out who he was. But being of short stature and because of the crowd, he could not see. So he ran ahead of the crowd and climbed into a sycamore-fig tree in order to catch sight of Jesus, since he was about to pass that way.

Having reached the spot, Jesus looked up and said, "Zacchaeus, hurry and come down. I must stay at your house today." So he hurried down at once and welcomed Jesus joyfully.

All who saw this began complaining, "He's gone to stay at a 'sinner's house."

But Zacchaeus stood up and said to the Lord, "Look, Lord! Here and now I give half of my possessions to the poor, and from whomever I've wrongly exacted anything, I'll pay back four times the amount."

Jesus said to him, "Today salvation has come to this house,

because this man, too, is a son of Abraham, indeed the Son of Man came to seek and to save that which was lost."

Salvation for Bartimaeus

As Jesus and his disciples were leaving Jericho, a sizeable crowd followed him. Two blind men, Bartimaeus (that is, the Son of Timaeus) and another, were sitting by the roadside begging. When they heard the crowd going by, they asked what was happening. When they were told that it was Jesus of Nazareth who was passing by, they shouted, "Lord, Jesus, Son of David, have mercy on us!"

The crowd rebuked them severely, telling them to be quiet, but they shouted all the louder, "Lord, Son of David, have mercy on us!"

Stopping, Jesus ordered the men to be brought to him. So they called to the blind men, "Cheer up! On your feet! He's calling you." Throwing off their cloaks, they sprang to their feet and came to Jesus.

"What do you want me to do for you?" Jesus asked.

"Lord," they answered, "we want our sight back."

Jesus had compassion on them and touched their eyes.

"Go on your way," he said, "receive your sight; your faith has healed you."

Immediately they recovered their sight and, praising God, followed Jesus along the road. When all the people saw it, they praised God also.

Home and away

While the crowd was listening to what Jesus was saying, he proceeded to tell them a parable, because he was near Jerusalem and the people were under the impression that the kingdom of God was going to appear immediately.

He said: "A certain man of noble birth was about to travel to a distant country to receive kingly authority, then to return. So he called his ten servants and entrusted his property to them, giving them each a sum of money according to his ability. For instance, to one he gave five portions, to another two and to another one. 'Conduct business,' he said, 'until I come back.' Then he went on his journey.

The man who had received the five portions went at once and put his money to work, gaining five more. So also the one with two portions gained two more. But the man who had received one portion went off, dug a hole in the ground and hid his master's money.

Now the noble man's own people hated him. They sent a delegation after him to say, 'We don't want this man to rule over us.'

Nevertheless he was made king and eventually returned home. Then he sent for the servants to whom he had given the money, in order to find out what they had gained by trading with it and to settle accounts.

The first one came and said, 'Master, you entrusted me with five portions, see I've gained five more.'

'Excellent, my good and faithful servant!' his master replied. 'Because you've been trustworthy in a very small matter, I'll put you in charge of many things – take charge of ten cities. Come and share your master's joy.'

Secondly, the man with the two portions came and said, 'Sir, you entrusted me with two portions, see I've gained two more.'

His master answered, 'well done good and faithful servant, you've been faithful with a few things; I'll put you in charge of many things. Take charge of five cities. Come and share your master's happiness.'

Then the servant who had received the single portion came and said, 'Master, here's your money; I wrapped it up in a piece of cloth and hid it in the ground. I was afraid of you, because you're an exacting man. You take out what you didn't deposit, gather where you haven't scattered and reap where you didn't sow.'

His master replied, 'I'll judge you by your own words, you wicked, lazy servant! You knew did you, that I'm a hard man, taking out what I didn't deposit, and reaping what I didn't sow? Why then didn't you put my money in the bank, so that when I came back, I could have collected it with interest?'

Then he said to those standing by, 'Take his money away from him and give it to the one who had ten times the amount.'

'Sir,' they said, 'he already has ten!'

He replied, 'I tell you that to everyone who has, more will be given, and they'll have an abundance. But from those who have nothing, even what they think they have, will be taken away.

Throw that worthless servant outside, into the darkness where there'll be weeping and gnashing of teeth. As for those enemies of mine who didn't want me to be king over them – bring them here and kill them in front of me.'"

After this, Jesus went on ahead, going up to Jerusalem.

It was now almost time for the Passover, so many people went up from the country to Jerusalem before the festival for their ceremonial cleansing. They kept looking for Jesus. As they gathered in the temple area they asked one another, "What do you think? Surely he isn't coming to the Feast?"

Now the chief priests and Pharisees had given orders that if anyone knew where Jesus was, it should be reported so that they might arrest him…

PART 3

The Last Week
The King is identified, rejected and crowned

*(It's worth remembering that biblical days ran from sunset to sunset.
This approximates to what is now generally known as 1800hrs/six o'clock
in the evening.)*

CHAPTER 17

Mainly Sunday

Saturday afternoon (9th Nisan)
Anointed at Bethany

Six days before the Passover, Jesus returned to Bethany.

There, in the home of a man known as Simon the Leper, a dinner was given in Jesus' honour. Lazarus, whom Jesus had raised from the dead, was among those reclining at the table with him. Martha was serving. Then Mary came to Jesus with an alabaster jar, holding about half a litre of very expensive perfume made of pure spikenard. Having broken the jar she poured it on Jesus' head and anointed his feet, wiping them with her hair. The house was filled with the fragrance of the perfume.

But Judas of Kerioth, objected, "Why wasn't this perfume sold and the money given to the poor? It was worth about a year's wages." (He didn't say this because he cared about the poor but because he was a thief and as keeper of the common purse he used to help himself to what was put into it.) When the other disciples saw what was happening, they too, along with some of those present, bristled with indignation saying, "Why this waste of perfume?" So they scolded her harshly.

Aware of this, Jesus said to them, "Why are you troubling this woman? Leave her alone. She has rendered a beautiful service to me. The poor you'll always have with you; you can help them whenever you want. But you won't always have me. Indeed, by

147

pouring this ointment, she has anointed my body beforehand for its burial. I tell you the truth, wherever the good news is proclaimed throughout the world, what she has done will also be told, in memory of her."

Meanwhile, a large crowd of Judeans found out that Jesus was there. They came, not only because of him but also to see Lazarus. So the chief priests, having taken counsel, made plans to kill Lazarus as well, for on account of him, many were deserting Judaism and turning to Jesus, putting their faith in him.

Sunday (10th Nisan)

The next day the great crowd that had come for the Feast heard that Jesus was on his way to Jerusalem.

Great expectations II

As Jesus and his disciples approached Jerusalem they came near to Bethphage, on the hill called the Mount of Olives. Jesus sent two of his disciples, saying to them, "Go into the village ahead of you, and at once you'll find a donkey tethered there, with her colt by her, that no-one has ever ridden. Untie them and bring them here to me. If anyone challenges you, tell them, 'the Lord needs them and will send them back here shortly'. The owner will send them straight away."

[This took place to fulfil what was spoken through the prophet:
'Say to the Daughter of Zion, do not be afraid.
See, your king comes to you, gentle and riding on a donkey,
on a colt, the foal of a donkey.']
The disciples went and did as Jesus had directed them.

Just as he had said, they found a donkey and colt tied securely to a door outside in the open street. As they untied them, some people standing there asked, "What are you doing, untying that colt?" They answered exactly as Jesus had told them to, so the people let them go.

When they brought the animals to Jesus the disciples threw their cloaks over the colt, then Jesus sat on it. Many from the crowd spread their cloaks on the road, while others cut branches from the trees in the fields, spreading the road with soft foliage.

When he came to the place where the road goes down the Mount of Olives, in loud voices, the whole crowd of disciples began to praise God joyfully for all the miracles they had seen.

Those in the crowd who had been with Jesus when he called Lazarus from the tomb and raised him from the dead, continued to spread this news. Many more people, because they had heard that Jesus had performed this miraculous sign, took palm branches and went out to meet him, shouting with the crowds that went ahead of him and those that followed:

"Hosanna to the Son of David!" "Hosanna in the highest!"
"Blessed is the King who comes in the name of the Lord!"
"Blessed is the King of Israel!"
"Blessed is the coming kingdom of our father David!"
"Peace in heaven and glory in the highest!"

(At first his disciples did not understand what was going on. It was only after Jesus was glorified that they remembered that these things had been written about him.)

As Jesus came near to Jerusalem and saw the city, he grieved over it, wailing loudly, "If you, even you, had only known on this day the things that make for real peace! But now it's hidden from your eyes. Alas the days will come upon you when your enemies will construct ramparts around you and will surround you, hemming you in on every side. You'll be dashed to the ground, you and your children. Not one stone will be left on another within your walls, because you didn't recognise the time that God visited you."

When Jesus entered Jerusalem, the whole city was in turmoil, asking, "Who on earth is this?"

The crowds responded, "This is Jesus, the prophet from Nazareth in Galilee."

Some of the Pharisees in the crowd said to Jesus, "Teacher, rebuke your disciples!"

"I tell you," he replied, "if they keep quiet, these very stones will cry out."

Exasperated, the Pharisees said to one another, "We're not gaining anything here. Look! the whole world's gone after him!"

Seeking Greeks

Among those who were going up to worship at the Feast, there were some Greeks. They approached Philip, "Sir," they said, "We'd like to meet Jesus." Philip went to tell Andrew; then both of them went to tell Jesus.

Jesus responded, "The hour has come for the Son of Man to be glorified. The truth is that unless a grain of wheat falls into the ground and dies, it remains only a single seed; but if it dies, it produces a harvest. Whoever loves his life loses it, while whoever hates his life in this world will keep it for eternal life. Whoever serves me must follow me; and where I am, there will my servant be also. If anyone serves me, the Father will honour him.

But now my soul is troubled, and what shall I say? 'Father, save me from this hour'? No, it was for this very reason that I have come to this hour. Father, glorify your name!"

Then a voice came out of heaven, "I have glorified it, and will glorify it again." Some in the crowd that stood there and heard it said it had thundered; others said, "An angel has spoken to him".

Jesus said, "This voice was for your benefit, not mine. Now is the time for judgment on this world; now the ruler of this world will be thrown out. But I, when I'm lifted up from the earth, will draw all peoples to myself." He said this to indicate the kind of death he was about to die.

The crowd responded, "We've heard from the Law that the Messiah will remain for ever; how can you say it's necessary for the Son of Man to be lifted up? Who is this 'Son of Man' anyway?"

Jesus answered, "You're going to have the light among you just a little while longer. Walk while you have the light, before darkness overtakes you. People who walk in the dark don't know where they're going. Believe in the light while you have it, so that you may become children of light."

Stock market clash

Jesus then entered the temple area. In the temple courts he found men selling cattle, sheep and pigeons, others were sitting as money-changers. So, having made, out of cords, some kind of whip, he drove out the sheep and cattle along with all who were trading there. He scattered the coins of the money-changers, overturning their tables and the benches of those selling doves. He would not allow anyone to carry merchandise through the temple courts. To those selling pigeons he shouted, "Get these things out of here! How dare you make a market of my Father's house?"

To all of them he said "It's written, 'My house will be known as a house of prayer for all peoples' but you're making it a hive of prey for profiteers." (His disciples later remembered that it is written: 'Zeal for your house will consume me.')

Confronting Jesus, the Judean leaders demanded, "What sign can you perform to prove your authority to do all these things?"

Jesus answered, "Destroy this temple, and I'll raise it up again in three days."

The Judeans replied, "This temple was under construction for forty-six years, and you'll raise it in three days?" (But Jesus had spoken of the temple of his body. After he was raised from the dead, his disciples remembered what he had said – so they believed the Scripture and the words that Jesus had spoken.)

The chief priests and the teachers of the law heard this and began looking for a way to destroy him, for they feared him, because the whole crowd was astonished at his teaching.

The excluded included

Blind and crippled people came to Jesus in the temple, so he healed them. But when the chief priests and the teachers of the law saw the wonders he performed, and the children crying out in the temple, "Hosanna to the Son of David," they were indignant. "Do you hear what these children are saying?" they asked him. "Yes," replied Jesus, "have you never read, 'From the lips of children and nursing babies you have prepared praise'?" Although Jesus had done all these miraculous signs in their presence, they still would not believe in him.

[This fulfilled the word of Isaiah: 'Lord, who has believed our message and to whom has the arm of the Lord been revealed?' Isaiah said this because he saw Jesus' glory and spoke about him.]

Believers

Nevertheless, at that time, even from among the leaders, many believed in him. But because of the Pharisees they would not confess their faith lest they be put out of the synagogue; for they loved praise from men more than praise from God.

Then Jesus cried out, "Whoever believes in me doesn't believe in me only, but in the one who sent me. Whoever sees me sees the one who sent me. I've come into the world as light, so that no-one who believes in me should remain in darkness.

If a person hears my words but doesn't keep them, I don't judge them. I didn't come to judge the world, but to save it. There's a judge for those who reject me and don't accept my words; the very words which I spoke will condemn them on the last day. I haven't spoken on my own authority, but the Father who sent me has himself commanded me what to say and how to say it. I know that his commands lead to eternal life. So whatever I say is precisely what the Father has told me to say."

Return to Bethany

When he had finished speaking, Jesus looked around, scrutinising everything, then left and hid himself from them. Since it was already late, with The Twelve, he went out of the city to Bethany, where they spent the night.

CHAPTER 18

Monday

11th Nisan
Fig leaves

Early in the morning of the next day, having left Bethany, on his way back to the city, Jesus was hungry. Seeing in the distance, by the road, a fig tree in leaf, he went to find out if it had any fruit. When he reached it, he found nothing on it but leaves, because it was not the season for figs. Then he said to the tree, "You won't bear fruit ever again; no-one will ever eat fruit from you again." His disciples heard him say this.

Whose authority?

When they arrived in Jerusalem, Jesus entered the temple courts. While he was walking around, teaching the people and preaching the good news, the chief priests and the teachers of the law, together with the elders of the people came up to him. "Tell us, by what right are you doing these things?" they asked[23]. "And who is it who gave you this authority?"

Jesus replied, "I'll also ask you one question. Answer me and I'll tell you by what authority I'm doing these things. Tell me, John's baptism – where did it come from? From heaven or from men?"

They discussed it among themselves saying, "If we say, 'From heaven,' he'll ask, 'Then why didn't you believe him?' But if we say, 'From men' well…" (They were afraid that all the people would stone them, because John was considered by them to be a genuine prophet.)

So they answered Jesus, "We don't know from where it came."

Well then he said, "Neither will I tell you by what authority I'm doing these things."

He went on, "What do you think? There was a man who had two sons. He went to the first and said, 'Son, go and work in the vineyard today.' 'I won't,' he answered, but afterwards he changed his mind and went. Then the father went to the other son and said the same thing. He answered, 'I'll go, sir,' but he didn't go.

Which of the two did the will of his father?"

"The first," they answered.

Jesus said to them, "I tell you the truth, the tax collectors and the prostitutes are entering the kingdom of God ahead of you. John came to you to show you the way of righteousness, yet you didn't believe him; but the tax collectors and the prostitutes did. Even after you saw this, you didn't repent later and believe him.

Tenants are us?

He then began to speak to the people in parables:

"Listen to another parable. There was a landowner who planted a vineyard. He put a fence around it, dug a pit for a winepress and built a watchtower. He leased the vineyard to some tenant farmers then went on a journey to another country for a long time. When harvest time approached, he sent his servants to the tenants, to collect from them some of the fruit of the vineyard.

But the tenants seized him, beat him and sent him away empty-handed.

Again he sent another servant to them; they struck this man on the head, treated him shamefully then sent him away empty-handed.

He sent still a third; they wounded him by stoning, then threw him out.

He sent still another; that one they killed.

Many other servants were sent to them but the tenants treated them the same way: some of them they beat, others they killed.

Finally the owner of the vineyard said, 'What shall I do? I have one last resort, I'll send my son, my darling whom I love; surely they'll respect him.' So last of all, he sent his son to them.

But when the tenants saw the son, they talked the matter over amongst themselves saying, 'This is the heir. Come, let's kill him and the inheritance will be ours.' So they took him, threw him out of the vineyard and killed him.

Now then, when the owner of the vineyard comes, what will he do to those tenants?

He'll come and kill those wretched tenants and give the vineyard to other tenants who'll give him his share of the crop at harvest time."

When the people heard this, they interjected saying, "Surely not, may this never be!"

Jesus looked directly at them and asked, "Then what's the meaning of that which is written in the Scriptures, have you never read:

'The stone the builders rejected has become the cornerstone;
the Lord has done this, and it is marvellous in our eyes'?

Therefore I tell you that the kingdom of God will be taken away from you and given to a people who'll produce its fruit. Everyone who falls on this stone will be broken to pieces; anyone on whom it falls will be crushed."

When the chief priests and the Pharisees heard his parables, they knew he was talking against them. Although they looked for a way to arrest him immediately, they were afraid of how the crowd might react. So they left him and went away.

Entrapment

Later, having watched Jesus closely, the Pharisees sent their disciples along with the Herodians as spies, pretending to be honest enquirers. They hoped to catch him in something he said, to ensnare him by his own statements, so that they might hand him over to the power and authority of the governor. So the spies questioned him: "Teacher, we know you're a man of integrity, you speak and teach what is right and you don't show partiality. You aren't swayed by men, because you pay no attention to who they are; but you teach the way of God in accordance with the truth. Tell us then, what's your opinion? Is it permissible for us to pay poll taxes to Caesar or not? Should we pay or shouldn't we?"

But Jesus knew their cunning evil intent and seeing through their duplicity said to them, "You hypocrites! Why are you trying to trap me? Bring me a coin used for paying the tax and let me look at it."

They brought the coin, and he asked them, "Whose image is this? Whose inscription is on it?"

"Caesar's," they replied.

He said to them, "Then pay to Caesar what is due to Caesar and to God what is due to God."

So they were unable to trap him in what he had said there in public. After standing gaping, astonished by his answer, they went away.

A resurrection issue

That same day some of the Sadducees came to Jesus with a question. "Teacher," they said, "Moses wrote telling us that if a man dies without having children, his brother must marry the widow and have children for him. Now there were seven brothers. The first one married and died, but because he had no children, he left his wife to his brother. The second one married the widow, but he also died childless. It was the same with the third brother, right on down to the seventh. In fact, none of the seven left any offspring. Finally, the woman died too. At the resurrection when they rise again, whose wife will she be, since all of the seven were married to her?"

Jesus replied, "You're in error because you neither know the Scriptures nor even the power of God. The people of this age marry and are given in marriage. But those who are considered worthy of taking part in that future age and in the resurrection from the dead, will neither marry nor be given in marriage; they can no longer die but will be like the angels in heaven. They're God's children, since they're children of the resurrection. But as for the resurrection of the dead – haven't you read in the book of Moses what God said to him in the account of the bush, 'I am the God of Abraham, the God of Isaac, and the God of Jacob'? You're badly mistaken! He isn't the God of the dead but of the living, for to him all are alive."

When the crowds heard this, they were astonished at his teaching.

The greatest commandment

Hearing that Jesus had silenced the Sadducees, the Pharisees came together.

One of them, a lawyer, came and heard them debating. Recognising that Jesus had given them a good answer, he tested him with this question, "Of all the commandments in the Law, which is the greatest, the most important?"

"The most important one" answered Jesus, "is this: 'Hear, O Israel, the Lord our God, the Lord is one. You shall LOVE the Lord your God with all your heart and with all your soul and with all your mind and with all your strength.' This is the first and greatest commandment. The second is like it: 'You shall love your neighbour as yourself.' There is no commandment greater than these. All the Law and the Prophets hang on these two commandments."

"Well said, teacher," the man replied. "You're right in saying that God is one and there is no other but him. To love him with all your heart, with all your understanding and with all your strength, and to love your neighbour as yourself is more important than all burnt offerings and sacrifices."

Seeing that he had answered wisely, Jesus said, "You aren't far from the kingdom of God."

While Jesus was teaching in the temple courts, the Pharisees were huddled together, Jesus asked them a question, "What do you think about the Messiah? Whose son is he?"

"The son of David," they replied.

He said to them, "How is it then that the teachers of the law say that the Messiah is the son of David yet David, speaking by the Holy Spirit, calls him 'Lord'? For he declared in the Book of Psalms:

'The Lord said to my Lord: 'Sit at my right hand until I put your enemies under your feet.'

If then David himself calls him 'Lord,' how can he be his son?"

No-one could say a word in reply. From that day on no-one dared to ask him any more questions. Yet the large crowd listened to him with delight.

Every day Jesus was teaching at the temple. However the chief priests, the teachers of the law and the leaders of the people kept looking for how they might destroy him. But they could not find any way to do it, because all the people hung on his words.

When evening came, Jesus and his disciples went out of the city to spend the night on the Mount of Olives, since all the people were coming early in the morning to hear him at the temple.

CHAPTER 19

Tuesday

12th Nisan
Fig tree faith

In the clear light of morning, as they went along, they saw the fig tree completely withered from the roots. Peter remembered and said to Jesus, "Rabbi, look! The fig tree that you cursed has withered away!"

When the disciples saw this, they were amazed. "How did the fig tree wither so quickly?" they asked.

"Keep having God-like faith," Jesus answered. "I tell you the truth, if you have faith and don't doubt in your heart, not only can you do what was done to the fig tree, but you also can say to this mountain, 'Be lifted up and throw yourself into the sea,' and it will be done. If anyone doesn't doubt, but believes that what they say will happen, it will be done for them. Therefore I'm telling you, whatever things you ask for in prayer, believe that you have received them, and they will be yours. And when you stand praying, if you hold anything against anyone, forgive them, in order that your Father in heaven may forgive you your sins."

Conspiracy afoot

Now the Passover and the Feast of Unleavened Bread were only two days away, so the chief priests and the teachers of the law assembled in the palace of the high priest, Caiaphas. They were looking for some way to be rid of Jesus, but they were afraid of the people. So they plotted for some sly way to seize Jesus and have him put to death. "But not during the Feast," they said, "or there may be a riot among the people."

The wedding party

On reaching Jerusalem Jesus spoke to them again in parables, saying:

"The kingdom of heaven is like a king who prepared a wedding reception for his son. He sent out his servants to call those who'd been invited to the banquet, but they didn't want to come.

Again he sent out some other servants saying, 'Tell those who've been invited that I've prepared my meal. My oxen and fattened cattle have been slaughtered, everything is ready. Come to the wedding banquet.'

But they made light of it and went their own way – one to his field, another to his business. The rest seized his servants, mistreated them and killed them. The king was enraged so he sent his army and destroyed those murderers and burned their city.

Then he said to his servants, 'The wedding banquet is ready, but those I invited didn't deserve to come. Go to the crossroads and invite to the wedding reception anyone you find.' So the servants went out into the streets and gathered everyone they could find, both good and bad. Thus the wedding hall was filled with guests.

But when the king came in to look over those reclining at the tables, he noticed a man there who wasn't wearing wedding clothes. 'My friend,' he asked, 'how did you enter in here without wedding clothes?' The man was speechless.

Then the king told the servants, 'Bind his hands and feet and throw him into the outer darkness, where there'll be weeping and grinding of teeth.'

For many are called, but few are chosen."

Blind leaders

While he was teaching, Jesus said to the crowds and to his disciples, "Always be wary of the teachers of the law and the Pharisees. They sit in Moses' seat, so you must obey them and do everything they tell you. But don't do what they do, because they don't practise what they preach. They devour widows' houses; for pretence they offer lengthy prayers. Such men will receive greater condemnation.

Everything they do is done for people to see. They like to walk around in flowing robes with their broad phylacteries and long tassels on their garments. They're fond of having the places of honour at banquets, and to have men call them 'Rabbi.'

But you aren't to be called 'Rabbi,' for you've only one teacher, and you're all brothers. Don't call anyone on earth 'father,' for you've one Father, your Heavenly Father. Nor are you to be called 'teacher,' for you've one Teacher, the Messiah.

The greatest among you will be your servant. Whoever exalts himself will be humbled, but whoever humbles himself will be exalted.

Woe betide you, teachers of the law and Pharisees, you hypocrites! You travel over land and sea to win one convert. But when they become one, you make them twice as much a son of hell as you are!

Woe betide you, blind guides! You say, 'If anyone swears by the temple, it means nothing; but if anyone swears by the gold of the temple, he's bound by his oath.' You blind fools! Which is greater: the gold, or the temple that makes the gold sacred? You say, 'If anyone swears by the altar, it means nothing; but if anyone swears by the gift upon it, they're bound by their oath.' You blind men! Which is greater: the gift, or the altar that makes the gift sacred? So whoever swears by the altar swears by it and by everything on it. And whoever swears by the temple swears by it and by the one who dwells in it. Whoever swears by heaven swears by God's throne and by the one who sits on it.

Woe betide you, teachers of the law and Pharisees, you hypocrites! You're like whitewashed tombs, which look beautiful on the outside but on the inside they're full of dead men's bones and all kinds of filth. In the same way, on the outside, you appear to people as righteous but on the inside you're full of hypocrisy and lawlessness.

"You snakes! You offspring of vipers! How can you escape being condemned to hell?"

Judging nations

"When the Son of Man comes in his glory, and all the angels with him, then he'll sit on his throne in heavenly splendour. All the nations will be assembled before him. He'll separate them, one from another as a shepherd separates the sheep from the goats. He'll put the sheep on his right, the goats on his left.

Then the King will say to those on his right, 'Come, you who've been blessed by my Father, inherit the kingdom which has been prepared for you since the creation of the world. For I was hungry and you gave me something to eat, I was thirsty and you gave me a drink, I was a stranger and you invited me in, I was naked and you clothed me, I was sick and you visited me, I was in prison and you came to see me.'

Then the righteous ones answered him, 'Lord, when did we see you hungry and feed you, or thirsty and gave you something to drink? When did we see you a stranger and invite you in, or naked and clothed you? And when did we see you sick or in prison and visited you?'

The King will reply, 'Truthfully, in as much as you did it for one of the least of my family, you did it for me.'

Then he'll say to those on his left, 'You who've been cursed, go away from me, into the eternal fire prepared for the devil and his angels. I was hungry but you didn't give me anything to eat. I was thirsty but you didn't give me a drink. I was a stranger but you didn't invite me in, naked but you didn't clothe me. I was sick and in prison but you didn't visit me.'

They will answer saying, 'Lord, when did we see you hungry, or thirsty, or a stranger, or needing clothes, or sick, or in prison, but didn't help you?'

He'll reply, 'I tell you truthfully, in as much as you didn't do it for one of the least, you didn't do it for me.'

Then they'll go away into eternal punishment, but the righteous into eternal life."

When Jesus had finished saying all these things, he said to his disciples, "As you know, the Passover is two days away – the Son of Man is about to be handed over to be crucified."

The betrayal

Then Satan entered Judas of Kerioth. He went to the chief priests and the officers of the temple guard for the purpose of discussing with them how he might betray Jesus to them.

Judas asked, "What are you willing to give me if I hand him over to you?" On hearing this, they were delighted and agreed to give him money. So they counted out for him thirty silver coins. From then on Judas was watching for a good opportunity, when no crowd was present, to hand Jesus over to them.

CHAPTER 20

Wednesday – Watch!

13th Nisan
Morning

As the first day of the *Feast of Unleavened Bread*[24] approached, when it was customary to sacrifice the Passover lamb, the disciples came to Jesus and asked, "Where do you want us to go to make preparations for you to eat the Passover?"

So he sent Peter and John, saying, "Go into the city, as you enter take note: a certain man carrying a pitcher of water will meet you. Follow him to the house that he enters, and say to the owner of the house, 'The Teacher says: My appointed time is near. Where, in your house, is my guest room where I may eat the Passover with my disciples?' He himself will show you a large upper room with couches already spread. Make preparations for us there."

The disciples did as Jesus had directed them: they left, went into the city and found things just as Jesus had told them. So they prepared the Passover.

Afternoon?
Giving all

Jesus sat down opposite the place where the offerings were placed and, with discerning eye, watched the crowd throwing their money into the temple treasury. As he looked, Jesus saw the wealthy people throwing in large amounts. But he also saw a poverty-stricken widow who came and put in two very small copper coins (worth only a fraction of a penny).

Calling his disciples to him, Jesus said, "I tell you truthfully, this poverty-stricken widow has put more into the treasury than all the others. All these people gave out of their plenty; but she out of her paucity has put in everything – all she had to live on.""

Coming destruction

Jesus left the temple and as he walked away, one of his disciples said to him, "Look, Teacher! What massive stones! What magnificent structures!" Other disciples were remarking about how the temple was adorned with beautiful stones and with gifts dedicated to God.

But Jesus replied, "Do you see all these great buildings? I tell you the truth about what you see here: the time will come when they'll all be demolished; not one stone will be left on another; every one of them will be thrown down."

Figuring it out

As Jesus was sitting on the Mount of Olives opposite the temple, Peter, James, John and Andrew came to him privately, "Teacher, tell us," they asked, "When will these things happen? What will be the sign that they are about to take place? What will be the distinguishing sign of your coming and the end of the age?"

The future – Jerusalem

Jesus answered, "When you see Jerusalem being surrounded by

armies, you'll know that its devastation is near. When you see standing in the holy place, where it doesn't belong, 'the abomination that causes desolation,' spoken of by the prophet Daniel. Then let those who are in Judea flee to the mountains, let those in the city leave, and let those in the country not enter the city.

This is the time of vengeance, in fulfilment of all that's been written. How dreadful it'll be in those days for pregnant women and nursing mothers! Pray that your flight won't take place in winter nor on the Sabbath.

There'll be great distress in the land, and wrath against this race. The people will fall by the sword and will be taken as prisoners to all the nations. Jerusalem will be trampled on by the nations until the times allotted to the nations are fulfilled."

The future – nations and followers

Then he said to them, "Always be watchful so that no-one deceives you or leads you astray. Many people will come using my name, claiming, 'I am the Messiah,' and, 'the time is near' and they will deceive many. Don't follow them.

You'll hear of revolutions, wars and rumours of wars, but see to it that you are neither afraid nor alarmed. These things must happen first, but the end won't come yet.

Nation will rise against nation, and kingdom against kingdom. There'll be great earthquakes, famines and pestilences in various places, terrifying events and great signs from heaven. All these are the beginning of intolerable anguish.

You must be constantly on your guard; before all this you'll be handed over to be persecuted by the local councils and flogged in the synagogues, delivered to prisons and put to death. You'll be hated by all nations because of me.

Because of my name you'll be brought before kings and governors as witnesses to them.

Whenever you're arrested and brought to trial, settle it in your mind not to worry. Do not prepare beforehand what to say nor how you'll defend yourselves. Simply say whatever is given you at the time, because it isn't you speaking, but the Holy Spirit. You'll be my mouthpiece. I'll give you words and wisdom that none of your adversaries will be able to resist nor contradict.

At that time many will fall away from the faith. They will betray and hate one another. You'll be betrayed even by parents, brothers, relatives and friends. Brother will betray brother to death and a father his child. Children will rebel against their parents and they'll put some of you to death. But not a hair of your head will perish.

Because of the increase of wickedness and lawlessness, the love of many will grow cold. Yet those who stand firm to the end will be saved, gaining LIFE, and this gospel of the kingdom will be proclaimed throughout the whole world as a testimony to all nations. Then the end will come.

There'll be days of great distress, unequalled from the beginning, when God created the world, until now – never to be equalled again. On the earth, nations will be in anguish and perplexity at the roaring and tossing of the sea. People's hearts will fail from fear of terror; being apprehensive of what is coming on the world. Immediately after the tribulation of those days the powers of the heavens will be shaken, there'll be signs in the sun, moon and stars:

The sun will be darkened, the moon won't give its light and the stars will fall from the sky.

If the Lord hadn't cut short those days, no-one would have survived, so for the sake of the elect, whom he has chosen, those days will be shortened. At that time if anyone says to you, 'Look, here is the Messiah!' or, 'There he is!' don't believe it. Indeed, false messiahs and false prophets will appear, performing great signs and miracles, deceiving many people, even the elect – if that were possible. So be ever on your guard; see, I've told you everything ahead of time.

If anyone tells you, 'There he is, out in the desert,' don't go out;

or, 'Here he is, in the inner rooms,' don't believe it. Because as lightning that comes from the east is visible even in the west, so will be the future appearing of the Son of Man.

At that time people will see the sign of the Son of Man appearing in the sky, and all the peoples of the earth will mourn. They'll see the Son of Man coming in clouds with great power and great glory. Then he'll send his angels with a loud trumpet call, and they'll gather his elect from the four winds, from the ends of the earth and from one end of the heavens to the other.

When these things begin to take place, stand up straight and lift up your heads, because your redemption is drawing near."

Fig leaf lesson

He told them this parable: "Now learn this lesson from the fig tree (and all the trees): As soon as its twigs become tender and it sprouts leaves, you know from experience that summer is near. Even so, when you see all these things happening, you know that the kingdom of God is near and the Son is right at the door. Truthfully I tell you, this race certainly won't pass away until all these things have happened. Heaven and earth will pass away, but my words will never pass away.

So watch yourselves, lest your hearts become weighed down with over-indulgence in sensual pleasures, nauseous drunkenness and the anxieties of life. Watch yourselves lest that day catches you unaware like a trap; because it will certainly come upon all those who live on the face of the whole earth. Therefore stay watchful at all times and pray, that you may be able to escape all that's about to take place, and that you may be able to stand before the Son of Man.

But concerning that day; no-one knows the day nor the hour, not the angels in heaven, nor even the Son, but only the Father. Therefore keep watch, stay awake! Be alert, because you don't know on what day your Lord will come. But understand this: If the owner of the house had known at what time of night the thief was coming, he would have kept watch and wouldn't have allowed his house to be broken into. So you too must be ready, because the Son of Man will come at an hour when you don't expect him."

Be ever ready

"Be suitably dressed ready for unhindered service. Keep your lamps burning, like men waiting for their master to return from a wedding reception, so that when he comes, and having knocked, they can immediately open the door for him. Those servants are blessed, whose master finds them watching when he comes. Truthfully, I tell you he'll dress himself to serve them. He'll have them recline at the table and will come himself and wait on them. If he comes after midnight, those servants will be truly blessed if their master finds them ready at that time. You also must be prepared, because the Son of Man will come when you don't expect him."

Peter asked, "Lord, are you only telling this parable to us, or to everyone else also?"

The Lord answered, "It's like a man who'd gone away to another country. He'd left his house and put his servants in charge of his household, each with his assigned task. He'd told the one at the door to keep watch and another to give food rations at the proper time.

Who then is the faithful and wise servant whom the master finds doing his allotted task when he returns? I tell you the truth, blessed is that servant, he'll be appointed to be in charge of all his possessions. But suppose that servant is wicked and begins to beat the other servants, saying to himself, 'My master is delaying his return,' And he begins eating and drinking to excess with drunkards. Look! On a day when he doesn't expect him and at an hour when he's unaware, the master of that servant will come. The master will cut the servant in pieces and assign him, with the unbelievers, to a place where there'll be weeping and gnashing of teeth.

That servant who, knowing his master's will, but neither

prepares nor does what his master wants, will be beaten severely. But the one who doesn't know, yet does things deserving punishment, will be beaten more lightly. From those who've been given much, much will be required; from those who've been entrusted much, much more will be asked of them.

Therefore keep watch because you don't know when the owner of the house will come back – whether in the evening, or at midnight, or when the rooster crows, or at dawn. If he comes suddenly, don't let him find you sleeping. What I say to you, I say to everyone: 'Watch!'"

Virgins' oil

"At that time the kingdom of heaven will be like ten virgins who took their lamps and went out to meet the bridegroom. Five of them were foolish, five were wise. When the foolish ones took their lamps, they didn't take enough oil with them. The wise, however, took extra oil in flasks along with their lamps. Since the bridegroom was a long time in coming, they all became drowsy and slept.

Then, at midnight, the cry rang out: 'Here comes the bridegroom! Come out to meet him!'

Immediately all the virgins woke up and trimmed their lamps. The foolish ones said to the wise, 'Give us some of your oil; our lamps are going out.'

'No,' they replied, 'there won't be enough for both us and you. Instead, go to the oil dealers and buy some for yourselves.'

While they were on their way to buy the oil, the bridegroom arrived. Those virgins who were ready went in with him to the wedding banquet. Then the door was shut.

Later the others virgins arrived. 'Lord! Lord!' they said. 'Open the door for us!'

But he replied, 'Truly, I don't know you.'

Therefore be vigilant, because you neither know the day nor the hour."

CHAPTER 21

Wednesday – Evening Meal

From 6 pm; start of 14th Nisan

When evening came, just before the *Passover Feast*[25] itself began, Jesus arrived at the house with The Twelve. He knew that he had come from God and the time had come for him to leave this world and return to the Father. Having loved his own who were in the world, he would now show them the utter extremity of his LOVE.

Jesus said to them, "At last my longing, to eat this Passover with you before I suffer, is satisfied. I tell you, I won't eat it again until it finds fulfilment in the kingdom of God."

Who's the greatest?

However, always loving contention, the disciples began arguing as to which of them was to be regarded as the greatest. Jesus said to them, "The kings of the nations lord it over them; and those who exercise authority over them claim the title of Benefactor. But you aren't to be like that. Instead, the greatest among you should be like the youngest, and the one who's chief like the one who serves. Who is greater, the one who is eating at the table or the one who serves? Isn't it the one who's at the table? But I'm among you as one who serves.

You're those who've persistently stood by me in my trials. So now I make a covenant of authority with you, in the same way as my Father has covenanted authority on me, in order that you may eat and drink at my table in my kingdom and sit on thrones, ruling the twelve tribes of Israel."

The servant king

The evening meal was in progress, with Jesus reclining at the table with the disciples. Then, knowing that the Father had put all things into his hands, Jesus got up from the meal and put aside his outer clothing. Taking a towel, he tied it around his waist. Then, having poured water into a basin, he began washing his disciples' feet, wiping them with the towel.

He came to Simon Peter who said to him, "Lord, are you going to wash my feet?"

Jesus answered, "You don't realise now what I'm doing, but later you'll understand."

"No," said Peter, "you'll never ever wash my feet."

Jesus answered, "Unless I wash you, you've no share in my destiny."

"Then, Lord," Simon Peter replied, "not only my feet but my hands and my head as well!"

Jesus replied, "A person who's had a bath doesn't need to wash except their feet; their whole body is clean. You're clean, though not every one of you." (He knew who was betraying him, so that was why he said not everyone was clean.)

When he had finished washing their feet, he put his clothes back on and reclined again at the table. "Do you understand what I've done for you?" he asked them. "You call me 'Teacher' and 'Lord,' and rightly so, for that's what I am. Now if I, your Lord and Teacher, have washed your feet, you also should wash one another's feet. I've set you an example that you should do as I've done for you. Truthfully speaking, a servant isn't greater than his master, nor is a messenger greater than the one who sent him. Now that you know these things, you'll be blessed if you do them. I tell you the truth, whoever welcomes anyone I send welcomes me; and whoever welcomes me welcomes the one who sent me."

Betrayal revealed

After he had said this, Jesus was troubled in spirit and declared, "I tell you the truth, one of you is going to betray me – one who's eating with me. I'm not referring to all of you; I know those I've chosen. But this is to fulfil the scripture: 'He who ate my bread has lifted up his heel against me.' I'm telling you now before it occurs, so that when it does happen you'll believe that I am He."

His disciples looked at one another, at a loss to know of which of them he spoke. Sorrowfully they began to question among themselves which of them it might be who would do this. One by one they said to him, "Surely not I Lord, is it?"

One of them, the disciple whom Jesus loved, was reclining next to him. Simon Peter nodded to this disciple and said, "Ask him which one he means."

Leaning back against Jesus, he asked him, "Lord, who is it?"

Jesus answered, "It's one of you twelve – the one who dips his hand into the deep dish with me and to whom I'll give this piece of bread when I've dipped it. The hand of him who's going to betray me is with mine on the table. The Son of Man will go exactly as it's been written and decreed about him. But alas for that man through whose agency the Son of Man is betrayed. It would be better for that man if he'd not been born."

Then Judas, the one who would betray him, said, "Surely not I, Rabbi?"

Jesus answered, "You've said it."

Then, dipping the piece of bread, he gave it to Judas, the son of Simon of Kerioth.

After Judas took the piece, Satan entered into him.

"What you're going to do, do quickly," Jesus told him, but no one at the meal understood why Jesus said this to him. Since Judas had charge of the purse, some thought Jesus was telling him to buy what was needed for the Feast, or to give something to the poor. So immediately the man had taken the bread, he went out. And it was night.

The new covenant

When he was gone out, Jesus said, "Now is the Son of Man glorified and God is glorified in him. If God is glorified in him, God will glorify the Son in himself, and will glorify him at once."

While they were eating, Jesus took *The Bread*[26] and gave a blessing. He broke the bread then gave it to his disciples, saying, "Take it; and eat; this is my body given for you; do this in remembrance of me."

In the same way, after the supper, having taken *The Cup,* he gave thanks and gave it to them saying, "Drink from it, all of you. This is my blood, the blood of the new covenant, which is being poured out on behalf of many for the forgiveness of sins. I tell you the truth: I'll definitely not drink again of the fruit of the vine from now on until that day when I drink the new quality wine with you in my Father's kingdom."

Then they all drank from The Cup.

A new commandment

Jesus continued, "A new command I give you: LOVE one another. Just as I've loved you; you must LOVE one another. By this everyone will know that you're my disciples, if you have LOVE amongst you.

My children, I'll be with you only a little longer. You'll look for me, but as I told the Judeans, so I tell you now: Where I'm going, you can't come."

Simon Peter asked him, "Lord, where are you going?"

Jesus replied, "Where I'm going, you can't follow now, but you'll follow later."

Peter asked, "Lord, why can't I follow you now?"

The way to the Father

Jesus answered, "Don't let your hearts be troubled. Trust in God; trust in me also. In my Father's house are many places to stay. If it weren't so, would I have told you that I'm going there to prepare a place for you? If I go to prepare a place for you, I'll come back and take you to be with me, so that you also may be where I am. You know the way to the place where I'm going."

Thomas said to him, "Lord, we don't know where you're going, so how can we know the way?"

Jesus answered, "I am the way and the truth and the LIFE. No-one comes to the Father except through me.

If you'd known me, you'd have known my Father already. From now you know him and have seen him."

Philip said, "Lord, show us the Father and that'll be enough for us."

Jesus answered: "Don't you know me, Philip, even after I've been with you such a long time? Those who've seen me have seen the Father. How can you say, 'Show us the Father'? Don't you believe that I am in the Father, and that the Father is in me? The words I say to you aren't just my own. Rather, it's the Father, living in me, who's doing his work. Believe me when I say that I am in the Father and the Father is in me; but if not, believe because of the miracles themselves.

I tell you the truth, anyone who believes in me will do what I've been doing. In fact they'll do even greater things than these, because I'm going to the Father. And I will do whatever you ask in my name, so that the Son may bring glory to the Father. If you ask for anything in my name, I will do it."

The coming Comforter

"If you LOVE me, you'll keep my commandments. I'm going to ask the Father, and he'll give you a Personal-Assistant, another *person exactly like me,* to be alongside of you forever – the Spirit of Truth. The world cannot receive him, because it neither sees him nor knows him. But you know him, because he lives with you and will be in you. I won't leave you as orphans; I'll come to you. In a short while the world won't see me anymore, but you'll see me. Because I live, you shall live also. On that day you'll realise that I'm in my Father, and you're in me, and I'm in you. Whoever has my commands and obeys them, he's the one who LOVES me. He who loves me will be loved by my Father and I too will love him and manifest myself to him."

Then Judas (son of James) said, "But, Lord, what's happened that you now intend to manifest yourself to us yet not to the world?"

Jesus replied, "If anyone loves me, they'll obey my teaching. My Father will love them and we'll come to them and make a place to stay with them. Whoever doesn't LOVE me won't obey my teaching. These words you hear aren't my own; they're from the Father who sent me.

All these things I've spoken to you while I'm still with you. But the Personal Assistant, the Holy Spirit, whom the Father will send in my name, he will teach you all things and remind you of everything I've said to you.

Peace I leave with you; my own peace I give you. I don't give to you the sort of peace the world gives. Don't let fear trouble your hearts neither let yourselves be intimidated.

You heard me say, 'I'm going away and I'm coming back to you.' If you loved me, you'd rejoice that I'm going to the Father, for the Father is greater than I. I've told you all this before it happens, so that when it does happen you'll believe. I won't speak with you much longer, for the ruler of this world is coming. He hasn't any claim on me, but in order that the world knows that I love the Father I do exactly what my Father has commanded me. Now let's arise and go from here."

So, having sung some psalms of praise, they went out to the Mount of Olives.

CHAPTER 22

Wednesday Night – Vintage Olivet

Jesus, according to his habit, went out to the Mount of Olives, and his disciples followed him.

Then he told them, "Tonight every one of you will be offended and desert me; it's written: 'I will strike the shepherd, and the sheep of the flock will be scattered.'

But after I've been raised, I will go ahead of you into Galilee."

Peter declared, "Lord, even if all are offended, I certainly never will desert you. I'm ready to go with you to prison and I will lay down my life for you."

Then Jesus answered, "Simon, Simon, will you really lay down your life for me? Listen, Satan has asked to sift you like wheat. But I've prayed for you, that your faith may not fail. When you've turned around, strengthen your brothers. Truthfully speaking Peter, I tell you, today – yes, this very night before the second *cock-crowing*[27] - three times you yourself will deny that you know me."

But Peter insisted vehemently, "Even if it's necessary for me to die with you, I'll never disown you." All the other disciples said the same.

Then Jesus asked them, "When I sent you out without purse, bag nor sandals, did you lack anything?"

"Nothing," they replied.

He said to them, "Well now, if you've a purse, take it, together with a bag. If you don't have a sword, sell your cloak and buy one. I tell you, it has been written, therefore it's necessary that it is fulfilled in me: 'And he was numbered with the lawless ones'. Yes, even these things concerning me must run their course."

The disciples said, "Look, Lord, here are two swords."

"That's enough," he replied.

The real vine

"I am the vine, the true one, and my Father is the vine-grower. He cuts off every branch of mine that isn't bearing any fruit, while every branch that is bearing fruit he prunes so that it'll bear even more fruit. You've already been pruned and made clean by the words I've spoken to you. Remain in me, and I'll remain in you. Since a branch can't bear fruit by itself unless it remains on the vine, neither can you bear fruit, unless you remain in me.

I am the vine; you're the branches. If a person continues to live in me and I in them, they'll bear much fruit; but apart from me you aren't able to do anything. If anyone doesn't continue living in me, they're like a dried up branch that, having dropped off, is picked up, thrown into the fire and burned. If you remain living in me and my words remain alive in you, you can ask whatever you wish, and it will be done for you. This is to my Father's glory, that you bear much fruit, showing yourselves to be my disciples."

Commanded to love

"As the Father has LOVED me, so I've loved you. Now continue to live in my love. If you keep my commands, you will continue to live in my love, just as I've obeyed my Father's commands and live in his love.

I've spoken these things to you so that my joy may be in you and that your joy may be made complete. This is my command: LOVE one another as I've loved you. Greater LOVE has no-one than this: that he lay down his life for his friends. You're my friends if you do the things I command. No longer do I call you servants, because a servant doesn't know what his lord is doing. But I've called you friends, because everything that I heard from my Father I've made known to you. You didn't choose me, but I chose you and appointed you to go and bear fruit – fruit that will last. Then whatever you ask the Father in my name he will give you. This is my command: LOVE one another."

Following the leader

"Remember the word I spoke to you: 'A servant isn't greater than his master'. If the world hates you, realise that it hated me first. If you belonged to the world, it would love you as its own. But you don't belong to the world, because I've chosen you out of the world. That's why the world hates you. If the people of the world persecuted me, they'll persecute you. If they keep my word they'll keep yours. They'll do these things to you on account of my name, because they don't know the one who sent me. If I hadn't come and spoken to them, they wouldn't be guilty of sin, but now they have no excuse for their sin. Whoever hates me hates my Father also.

If, while among them, I hadn't done the works which no-one else has done, they wouldn't be guilty of sin. But they've seen these miracles, yet still they've hated both me and my Father. This is to fulfil what's written in their Law: 'They hated me without a cause.'

I've spoken these things to you so that you won't be offended and stumble. They'll put you out of the synagogue; in fact, a time is coming when anyone who kills you will think they're offering a service to God. They'll do such things because they haven't known the Father nor me.

I've spoken these things so that when the time comes you'll remember that I warned you. I didn't tell you this from the beginning because I was with you."

More about the coming counsellor

"When the Personal-Assistant (the Spirit of Truth) comes, whom I'll send to you from the Father, he'll testify about me. Then you too will testify, because you've been with me from the beginning.

Now I'm going to the one who sent me, but only one of you asks me, 'Where are you going?' Yet because I've said these things, your hearts are filled with sorrow. So I'll tell you the truth: it's necessary, and it's to your benefit, that I go away. Unless I go, the Personal-Assistant won't come. But if I go, I'll send him to you.

When the Personal Assistant comes, he'll expose the world's concepts about sin, about having a right standing with God and about judgement.

He'll convict the world in regard to sin because people don't believe in me.

He'll convict the world in regard to having a right standing with God, because I'm going to the Father, where you can see me no longer.

He'll convict the world in regard to judgment, because the ruler of this world has been condemned.

I've many more things to say to you, but you can't bear them now. However when the Spirit of Truth has come, he himself will guide you in every truth. He'll not speak on his own initiative nor about himself; he'll speak only what he hears, and he'll disclose what's to come. He'll bring glory to me by taking from what is mine, proclaiming and explaining it to you. All things that belong to the Father are mine. That's why I said he *(the Spirit)* will take from what's mine and proclaim and explain it to you."

Returning to the Father

"In a little while you'll no longer see me, then after a little while you'll see me again."

Some of his disciples said to one another, "What's he talking about, 'In a little while you'll no longer see me, and then after a little while you'll see me again,' and 'Because I'm going to the Father'?" They kept asking, "What does he mean by 'a little while'? We don't understand what he's talking about!"

Jesus knew that they were wanting to ask him about this, so he said to them, "Are you asking one another what I meant when I said, 'In a little while you'll no longer see me, and then after a little while you'll see me again'? The honest truth is that you'll weep and mourn but the world will rejoice. You'll grieve, but your grief will be turned to joy. A woman giving birth has grief because her time has come; but when the baby is born she no longer remembers the suffering because of the joy that a child is born into the world. Similarly with you: you now grieve, but I will see you again and your hearts will rejoice, then no-one will be able to take away your joy. On that day you'll not ask me anything. The absolute truth is that, whatever you ask the Father in my name, he'll give it you. Until now you haven't asked anything in my name. Keep on asking and you'll receive, that your joy will be fulfilled.

I've spoken these things to you figuratively, but a time is coming when I'll no longer speak figuratively but I'll plainly proclaim to you things concerning my Father. In that day you'll ask in my name. I'm not saying that I'll ask the Father for you. No, the Father himself loves you because you've loved me and have believed that I came from God. Indeed I came from the Father and came into the world. Again, I say that I'm leaving the world and going back to the Father."

Then Jesus' disciples said, "Now you are speaking plainly and no longer using figures of speech. Now we know that you know all things, so there's no need for anyone to question you. Because of this we believe that you came from God."

"Do you believe at last?" Jesus answered. "Look, a time is coming, and has already come, when you'll be scattered; each to his own place, and you'll leave me alone. Yet I'm not alone, because the Father is with me.

I have spoken these things to you, so that in me you may have peace. In the world you'll have many sufferings, but take courage, I've conquered this world!"

CHAPTER 23

Wednesday Night – Gethsemane

The Lord's prayer

After Jesus had spoken to them, he lifted his eyes to heaven and prayed:

"Father, the time has come. Glorify your Son, that your Son may glorify you. You gave him authority over all people in order that he might give eternal life to all those you have given him. And this is eternal life: that they may know you, the only true God, and Jesus, the Christ, whom you sent. I've glorified you on earth by finishing the work you gave me to do. So now, Father, glorify me along with yourself with the glory I was experiencing with you before the world existed.

I've revealed your name to the men whom you gave me out of the world. They were yours; you gave them to me and they've kept your word. Now they know that everything you've given me is from you, because the words you gave me, I have given them, and they received them. They truly know now that I came from you, and they believe that you sent me. I ask, concerning them. I'm not asking for the world, but for these ones you've given me, because they're yours. Everything l have is yours, and everything you have is mine. Now glory has come to me through them.

I'll not remain in the world much longer, but they're still in the world, and I'm coming to you. Holy Father, keep them by the power of your name – the name you gave me – so that they may be one just as we are. While I was with them, I kept them in the power of that name you gave me. I kept watch: none has perished except the son of perdition, so that Scripture would be fulfilled.

Now I'm coming to you, and I say these things while I'm still in the world, so that the men you gave me may have my joy fulfilled within themselves. I've given them your word. The world has hated them, because they aren't of this world just as I'm not of the world. I'm not asking that you take them out of the world but that you protect them from the evil one. They aren't of the world, just as I'm not of the world. Set them apart for yourself in the truth; your word is truth. As you sent me into the world, I've also sent them into the world. I now consecrate myself on their behalf so they too may be truly set apart for you.

I'm not praying for these men alone. I'm praying also for those who'll believe in me through their words, that all of them may be one. Father, just as you're in me and I'm in you, may they also be in us so that the world may believe that you sent me. I've given them the glory that you gave me, that they may be one just as we are one: I in them and you in me. May they be brought to perfect unity so the world will know that you sent me and have loved them even as you've loved me.

Father, I desire that those you've given me will be with me where I am, and that they'll see my glory, the glory you've given me because you loved me before the foundation of the world.

Righteous Father, even though the world doesn't know you, I know you, and these men know that you've sent me. I've made your name known to them, and I'll keep on making you known, in order that I, and the LOVE with which you've loved me, may be in them."

In Gethsemane
The Lord prays again

When he had finished praying, Jesus, with his disciples, crossed the

Kidron wadi. On the other side there was a garden of fruit trees, a place called Gethsemane, which, on reaching, they entered.

Jesus said to his disciples, "Sit down here while I go over there and pray." Then taking Peter, James and John along with him, he began to be thoroughly alarmed and deeply distressed. He said to them, "My soul is overwhelmed with grief to the point of death. Remain here, stay awake and watch with me."

Withdrawing a little farther, about a stone's throw beyond them, he fell, with his face to the ground. He kept praying that if possible the hour might pass from him.

"Dearest Father," he was pleading, "Everything's possible for you. If you're willing, please remove this cup from me; yet it's not what I want myself, but what you want."

Then he returned to his disciples and found them sleeping. "Simon," he said to Peter, "are you sleeping? Weren't you men strong enough to keep watch with me for one hour? Keep watching and praying so that you won't fall into temptation. The spirit indeed is willing, but the body is weak."

For the second time, he went away and prayed the same words, "My Father, if it isn't possible for this cup to be taken away unless I drink it, let your will be done."

An angel from heaven appeared to him and strengthened him. Being in anguish, he prayed more fervently; his sweat became like drops of blood falling to the ground.

When he rose from prayer he went back to the disciples, again he found them asleep; their eyes were heavy because they were exhausted from sorrow. "Why are you sleeping?" he asked them. "Rise and pray so that you'll not fall into temptation." But they did not know how they should answer him.

So he left them and went away once more, praying a third time; saying the same words. Then he returned to the disciples and said to them, "Are you still sleeping and resting? Enough! The time has come. Look, the Son of Man is at this moment being betrayed into the hands of sinners. Rise! Let's go! My betrayer is close by!"

Extraordinary rendition?

Judas, the one of The Twelve who was betraying him, knew this place, because Jesus often gathered here with his disciples.

So, even as Jesus was speaking, Judas arrived leading a large crowd sent from the high priests, Pharisees, experts in the law and the elders of the people. The crowd included a *detachment of soldiers*[28i], some officers from the chief priests and Pharisees. They were carrying torches and lanterns, and were armed with swords and clubs.

Jesus, knowing all that was going to happen to him, stepped forward and asked them, "Who are you looking for?"

"Jesus of Nazareth," they replied.

"I am *he*," Jesus said. (Judas the traitor was standing there with them.) When Jesus said, "I am" they went backwards and fell to the ground.

Again he questioned them, "Who are you looking for?"

They said, "Jesus the Nazarene."

"I told you that I am *he*," Jesus answered. "If you're looking for me, then let these men go." This happened so that the words he had spoken would be fulfilled: 'I haven't lost any one of those you gave me.'

Now the betrayer had given them a pre-arranged signal: "The one I kiss is the man; arrest him and lead him away securely." So having arrived, Judas immediately approached Jesus, saying, "Greetings, Rabbi!" and kissed him fervently.

Jesus asked him, "Judas, my friend, would you betray the Son of Man with a kiss? Do what you came to do."

Then men stepped forward, seized Jesus and arrested him.

With that Simon Peter, who was standing near, drew his sword and struck the high priest's servant, cutting off his right ear. (The servant's name was Malchus.)

When Jesus' followers saw what was going to happen, they said, "Lord, should we strike with our swords?"

Jesus replied, "No more of this! Let events take their course." He touched the man's ear and healed him.

Jesus then commanded Peter, "Put your sword back into its sheath. Shouldn't I drink the cup the Father has given me? All who draw the sword will die by the sword. Do you think I can't call on my Father, and he'll at once put at my disposal more than twelve legions of angels? But how then would the scriptures be fulfilled that say it's necessary for it to happen in this way?"

At that time Jesus said to the chief priests, officers of the temple and the elders, in the crowd who had come for him, "Am I leading a rebellion that you've come out with swords and clubs to seize me? Day after day I sat with you in the temple teaching, yet you didn't arrest me or lay a hand on me. But this is your hour – when darkness reigns. It all is taking place that the prophetic scriptures might be fulfilled."

Then all the disciples deserted him and fled.

A certain young man, wearing nothing but a long linen shirt, was following Jesus. When the arresting party tried to seize this man, leaving his garment behind, he also ran away – naked.

CHAPTER 24

Thursday Morning

14th Nisan – early hours
Illegal Inquisition

Those who had seized Jesus bound him and led him first to Annas, who was the father-in-law of Caiaphas, the high priest that year. (It was Caiaphas who had counselled the religious Judeans that it would be expedient if one man died on behalf of the people.) Annas proceeded to question Jesus about his disciples and his teaching.

"I've spoken publicly to the world," Jesus replied. "I've always taught in synagogues or in the temple, where all Judeans come together. I've said nothing in secret. Why interrogate me? Ask those who heard me. They'll surely know what I said."

When Jesus said this, one of the officials standing nearby slapped him in the face. "Is this how you answer the high priest?" he demanded.

"If I've said something wrong," Jesus replied, "testify as to what's wrong. But if I spoke the truth, why did you strike me?"

Then Annas sent him, still bound, to the house of Caiaphas where all the chief priests had gathered, together with the teachers of the law and the elders.

A denial

Simon Peter and another disciple had been following Jesus at a distance. Because this disciple was an acquaintance of the high priest, he went with Jesus into the high priest's courtyard, but Peter had to stand waiting outside at the door.

It was cold, so to keep warm the servants and officials stood around a charcoal fire, they had kindled in the middle of the courtyard.

The other disciple, who was acquainted with the high priest, came back, spoke to the girl on door-keeping duty, then brought Peter in. He entered gingerly and sat down with the guards, by the fire, warming himself with them – waiting to see the outcome of events.

When a servant girl saw him, sitting there in the firelight, she stared at him and said, "Ah! Surely, you also were with that Nazarene, Jesus of Galilee."

But Peter denied it before them all, "Woman, I don't know him. I don't understand what you're talking about," he said.

The silence of the lamb

The chief priests and the whole Sanhedrin kept looking for false evidence against Jesus, with the intention of putting him to death. But they did not find any; although many false witnesses came forward, their statements did not tally.

Finally two came forward and gave this false testimony against him, declaring "We heard him say, 'I'll destroy this man-made temple and in three days rebuild another, not made by human hands.'" Yet even then their testimony was inconsistent.

Then the high priest stood up amongst them and said to Jesus, "Aren't you going to answer? What are these allegations these men are bringing against you?" But Jesus remained silent, giving no answer.

The high priest said to him, "I charge you under oath by the living God: Tell us if you are the Anointed King, the Son of the Blessed One."

Jesus replied, "If I tell you, you won't believe. But I say to all of you: from now on you'll see the Son of Man sitting at the right hand of the Mighty One and you'll see him coming on the clouds of heaven."

So all of them asked, "Are you then the Son of God?"

"Those are your words, not mine, but you're right, I cannot deny it," Jesus answered.

Then the high priest tore his tunic apart and said, "He has spoken blasphemy! Why do we need any more witnesses? Look, now you've heard it from his own mouth. What's your verdict?"

"He is guilty and worthy of death," they answered.

Then some, who were guarding Jesus, began mocking and beating him, spitting in his face; they blindfolded him and struck him with their fists. Others slapped him and said, "Prophesy to us, Messiah. Who hit you?" Reviling him, they said many other insulting things.

More denials

A little later, Peter, still below in the courtyard, went out to the doorway, where another servant girl saw him and said to the bystanders, "This man is one of them."

"You aren't one of his disciples, are you?" the girl asked Peter.

He denied it again, with an oath saying, "I'm not. I don't know the man!"

About an hour later (by now it was early morning), the whole company of the chief priests convened a council with the elders of the people, the teachers of the law and the entire Sanhedrin. They reached the decision to put Jesus to death.

They bound Jesus, and were leading him away from Caiaphas' house to the *Praetorium*[29], to hand him over to Pilate, the governor. Just then one of the high priest's servants, a relative of the man whose ear Peter had cut off, challenged Peter, "Didn't I see you with him in the olive grove?" Those standing there went up to Peter and were insisting, "Surely you're one of them; your Galilean accent gives you away."

Cursing and swearing, Peter denied it again saying, "Man, I don't know him! I don't know what on earth you're talking about."

At that moment, as he was speaking, a cock began to crow. The Lord turned and looked directly at Peter. Then Peter remembered the word the Lord Jesus had spoken to him: "Before the second cock-crowing today, you'll disown me three times."

He went outside, broke down, and wept bitterly.

Before Pilate

To avoid ceremonial uncleanness the Judean leaders did not enter the Praetorium themselves because they wanted to be able to eat the Passover. So Pilate came outside to them and asked, "What charges are you bringing against this man?"

"If he weren't committing crimes," they replied, "we wouldn't be handing him over to you."

So they began to accuse him, saying, "We've found this man subverting our nation, forbidding the payment of taxes to Caesar and claiming that he himself is the Messiah – a king."

Pilate said, "You take him yourselves and judge him by your own law."

"But we've no legal right to execute anyone," the Judeans objected. (This was to fulfil the words Jesus had spoken, signifying the manner by which he was going to die.)

The chief priests and the elders kept on accusing him of many things but he gave no answer. Then Pilate asked him, "Don't you hear the testimony they are bringing against you? See how many things they are accusing you of. Aren't you going to answer even one accusation?"

But, to the astonishment of the governor, Jesus made no reply; not even to a single charge.

Pilate then went back inside the Praetorium and summoned Jesus to stand before him asking, "Are you the king of the Judeans?"

"Yes, it's as you say," Jesus replied, "but are you asking that from your own reasoning or have others told you about me?"

"Am I a Judean?" Pilate responded. "It was your people and the High Priest who handed you over to me. What have you done?"

Jesus replied, "My kingdom isn't cut from the pattern of this world. If it were, my servants would have fought to prevent my arrest by the Judeans. But as it is my kingdom does not originate here."

"You *are* a king, then!" said Pilate.

Jesus answered, "'King' is your word and you are right in saying it. But the reason I was born and the reason I came into the world was to testify to the truth. Everyone on the side of truth listens to me."

"What is truth?" Pilate asked.

With this he went out again, He announced to the chief priests and the crowd, "I find no basis for a charge against this man."

But they insisted, "By his teaching he incites the people throughout the whole of Judea. He began in Galilee and has come all the way here."

Before Herod

On hearing this, Pilate asked whether the man was a Galilean. When he learned that Jesus came under Herod's jurisdiction, he sent him to Herod, who was also in Jerusalem at that time.

When Herod saw Jesus, he was delighted because, having heard about him for a long time, he had wanted to meet him. He hoped to see Jesus perform some miracle. Herod plied him at length with many questions, but Jesus gave him no answers. The chief priests and the teachers of the law were standing there, vehemently accusing him. Herod and his soldiers, having dressed him in a regal robe, ridiculed and mocked him. Then they sent him back to Pilate. That very day Herod and Pilate became friends – before this there had been enmity between them.

Pilate's pleas

Pilate then called together the chief priests, the rulers and the people, and said to them, "You brought me this man as a revolutionary. But look, I have examined him in your presence and have found nothing to substantiate your charges against him. Neither did Herod, because he sent him back to us. In fact, as you can see, he has done nothing to deserve the death penalty. Therefore, I'll chastise him and then release him."

Now it was the governor's custom at the Feast to release a prisoner chosen by the people. At that time they had a notorious prisoner, commonly called Jesus-Barabbas. He had been thrown into prison with other terrorists who had committed murder in an uprising which had occurred in the city. So having gathered the crowd, Pilate addressed them saying, "It's necessary that I release someone for you at Passover. Which one do you want me to release to you: Jesus-Barabbas, or Jesus, the King of the Judeans?" It had dawned on him that it was out of sheer envy that the chief priests had handed Jesus over to him.

But the chief priests and the elders stirred up the people, persuading the crowd to have Pilate release Barabbas, and have Jesus executed.

"Which of the two do you want me to release to you?" asked the governor again.

They cried out all together, "Away with this man! Release Barabbas! Give us Barabbas!"

"What shall I do, then, with him whom you are calling the Christ?" Pilate asked.

They all shouted, "Crucify him at once!"

"Why? What crime has he committed?" asked Pilate.

But they kept shouting all the louder, "Crucify him!"

Wanting to release Jesus, Pilate addressed them again. But they kept shouting,

"Crucify him! Crucify him!"

For the third time he appealed to them: "Why? What crime has this man committed? I have found in him no grounds for the death penalty."

But with loud voices they persistently insisted that he be crucified; and their shouts prevailed. So when Pilate saw that he was getting nowhere, but that instead uproar was starting, he took water and, in front of the crowd, washed his hands. "I'm innocent of this man's blood," he said. "It's your responsibility!"

All the people answered, "Let his blood be on us and on our children!"

Wanting to satisfy the crowd, Pilate decided to grant their request. He released to them Barabbas, surrendering Jesus to their will.

He then had Jesus *flogged*[30].

Judas's remorse

When Judas saw that Jesus had been condemned to death, he regretted his action so he returned the thirty silver coins to the chief priests and the elders. "I sinned," he said, "I've betrayed innocent blood."

"What's that to us?" they replied. "That's your problem."

So Judas defiantly threw down the silver in the temple. He went away and hanged himself.

The chief priests picked up the coins and said, "It's not permitted to put this into the treasury, it's blood money." So, having agreed with the elders, they used the money to buy the potter's field as a burial place for foreigners. That is why to this day it has been called the Field of Blood.

[Thus what was spoken by Jeremiah the prophet was fulfilled: 'They took the thirty silver coins, the price set on him by the people of Israel, and they used them to buy the potter's field, as the Lord commanded me'.]

Not guilty

Then the governor's soldiers led Jesus away into the courtyard of the Praetorium. They called the whole cohort of soldiers together around him, stripped him and threw a purple garment around him. Next they twisted thorns together into a victor's wreath and set it on his head. They put a reed in his right hand and falling on their knees in front of him, they mockingly paid homage to him.

They began to call out to him "Hail, King of the Judeans!" Again and again they slapped him, spat on him and kept beating him on the head with a staff.

Once more Pilate came out and said to the Judeans, "I'm bringing him out to you to let you know that I find no fault in him." When Jesus came out wearing the thorny wreath and the purple garment, Pilate said to them, "Look! Here is the man."

As soon as the chief priests and their officials saw him, they shouted, "Crucify! Crucify!"

But Pilate answered, "You take him and crucify him. As for me, I find no case against him."

The Judean leaders insisted, "We have a law, and according to that law he must die, because he claimed to be the Son of God."

When Pilate heard these words, he was afraid – very afraid, so he went back inside the Praetorium. "Where are you from?" he asked Jesus. But Jesus didn't give him an answer.

"Do you even refuse to speak to me?" Pilate retorted. "Don't you realise I have authority either to free you or crucify you?"

Jesus answered, "You don't have any authority over me at all unless it has been given to you from above. Therefore the one who handed me over to you is guilty of a greater sin."

From then on, Pilate tried to set Jesus free, but the Judeans kept shouting, "If you let this man go free, you are no friend of Caesar. Anyone who claims to be a king speaks against Caesar."

When Pilate heard this, he brought Jesus out and sat down on the judgment seat at a place known as the Mosaic Pavement, which in Aramaic is Gabbatha. (While Pilate was sitting there his wife sent him this message: 'Don't have anything to do with that innocent man, for I have suffered a great deal today in a dream because of him.')

"Here is your king," Pilate said to the Judeans.

But they shouted, "Take him away! Take him away! Crucify him!"

"Shall I crucify your king?" Pilate asked.

"We have no king except Caesar," the chief priests answered.

Finally Pilate succumbed to their will and sentenced him to be crucified.

So the soldiers took charge of Jesus. They removed the garment and put his own clothes on him. Then they led him away to crucify him.

It was the day of Preparation of Passover Week, about nine o'clock in the morning.

CHAPTER 25

Thursday – Mourning

14th Nisan, approx 9 a.m. to mid-day
The lamb is slaughtered

Jesus went out carrying his own cross.

As the soldiers were going, they seized and pressed into service a man named Simon, a Cyrenian. He was passing by on his way in from the surrounding countryside. (He was the father of Alexander and Rufus.) They put the cross on him and forced him to carry it, and follow Jesus.

A large multitude, including women who were mourning and lamenting, followed him. Jesus turned towards them saying, "Daughters of Jerusalem don't cry for me; cry for yourselves and for your children. For the days are coming when they'll say, 'Blessed are the barren, the wombs that never bore and the breasts that never nursed!' Then they'll begin to say to the mountains, 'Fall on us!' and to the hills, 'Bury us!' If people do these things when the tree is full of moisture, what will happen when it's dry?"

Two other men, both criminals, were led out with him to be executed.

They came to the place called 'The Skull' ('Golgotha' in Aramaic). Jesus was offered wine mixed with myrrh; but after tasting it, he refused to drink it.

There they crucified him, with the two freedom fighters – one on his right and one on his left.

He kept saying, "Father, forgive them, they don't know what they're doing."

Pilate had prepared a placard, on which was inscribed the charge against Jesus. It was fastened to the cross above Jesus' head. It said: This is JESUS OF NAZARETH, THE KING OF THE JUDEANS. Many Judeans read this title, because the place where Jesus was crucified was near the city. The inscription was written in Aramaic, Latin and Greek. The chief priests protested to Pilate, "Don't write 'The King of the Judeans,' but that this man said 'I am the king of the Judeans'."

Pilate answered, "What I have written, I have written."

When the soldiers had crucified Jesus, they took his clothes and divided them into four parts, one for each of them; with the undertunic remaining. This latter garment was seamless, woven in one piece from the top. "Let's not split it," they said to one another. "Let's decide by lot who'll win it." So they cast lots to see whose it would be.

[This happened so that the Scripture might be fulfilled which said, 'They divided my garments among them and cast lots for my clothing.']

Then they sat down and began keeping watch over him.

Despised and rejected

Those passing by, and the people who stood watching, mocked and insulted him. They shook their heads and said, "Ha! You, the one who was going to destroy the temple and build it in three days, save yourself! And if you're the Son of God, come down from the cross!"

Similarly the chief priests, the teachers of the law and the elders were sneering at him; mockingly among themselves they said, "He saved others, but he can't save himself! If he's the King of Israel, let this Messiah come down from the cross right now in order that we may see and believe in him. He has trusted in God; if he's pleased with him, let God rescue him now. After all he did say, 'I am the Son of God.'"

In the same way the freedom fighters taunted him.

The soldiers approached and ridiculed him too. They offered him wine-vinegar saying, "If you're the king of the Judeans, save yourself."

One of the criminals who hung there with him was blaspheming him and saying, "Aren't you the Messiah? Save yourself and us!"

But the other one rebuked him. "Don't you fear God," he said, "since you're under the same sentence? We're getting the just deserts for our transgressions. But this man did nothing wrong."

Then he said, "Jesus, remember me when you come into your kingdom."

Jesus replied to him, "I tell you the truth, today you will be with me in paradise."

Filial care

Standing near the cross of Jesus were his mother, his mother's sister, Mary the wife of Clopas, and Mary of Magdala. Having seen his mother and the disciple whom he loved, standing beside her Jesus said to his mother, "Dear woman, here is your son," and to the disciple, "Here is your mother." From that moment, the disciple took her into the care of his own household.

Mid-day to about 4 p.m.
Son eclipses sun

From mid-day until three in the afternoon a darkness came over the whole land because the sun's light was obscured.

About three o'clock Jesus cried out in a loud voice, "Eloi, Eloi, lama sabachthani?" – which means, "My God, my God, why have you abandoned me?"

On hearing this, some of those standing by said, "Listen, he's calling for Elijah."

Jesus dies

Afterwards, Jesus, knowing that everything had now been completed (i.e. that the scriptures would be fulfilled), said, "I am thirsty."

A jug of wine-vinegar was nearby. Immediately someone ran and found a sponge, soaked it with some of the vinegar, then having wrapped it around a stick from a hyssop plant he lifted it to Jesus' mouth. Others said, "No, hold off; let's see whether Elijah comes to take him down and save him."

When he had received the drink, Jesus cried out, "It is accomplished."

Then Jesus cried out again in a loud voice, "Father, into your hands I entrust my spirit." With that he laid his head to rest, and, surrendering his spirit, he breathed out his life.

At that moment the *curtain*[31] to the inner temple was torn in two from top to bottom.

The earth shook, rocks split, tombs broke open and the bodies of many holy people who had died were raised to life. After Jesus' resurrection they went into the holy city and appeared to many people.

When the centurion, who stood there in front guarding Jesus, heard his cry and saw how he died, he began praising God and saying, "Surely this man was innocent. Surely he was the son of God!"

When all the people who had gathered to witness this spectacle, experienced the earthquake and considered all that took place, they were terrified and returned to their homes, beating their breasts.

The relatives of Jesus and the women who had followed him from Galilee, to care for his needs, were watching attentively from a distance. Besides those mentioned already, were Mary the mother of James (the younger) and Joses, and Salome the mother of Zebedee's sons. Many other women who had come with him up to Jerusalem were there also.

Up to sunset – 14th Nisan
The burial

As it was the Day of Preparation, and the next day was to be a special Sabbath, the Judean leaders did not want any body left on a cross during the Sabbath. So they asked Pilate to have the legs broken and the bodies taken away. Therefore the soldiers came and broke the legs of the first man and then those of the other who had been crucified with Jesus. But on coming to Jesus and seeing that he was already dead, they did not break his legs. Instead, one of the soldiers pierced Jesus' side with a spear. Immediately blood and water poured out.

The man who saw this has testified to it, and his testimony is true. He knows that he tells the truth, and he testifies so that you also may believe.

[These things happened so that the scripture would be fulfilled: 'Not one of his bones will be broken.'
And again, a different scripture says: 'They will look on the one they have pierced.']

Afterwards, as evening approached, Joseph, a wealthy man from the Judean town of Arimathea, took courage. Boldly he approached Pilate to ask for the body of Jesus. Joseph was a reputable member of the Council. He was a good and upright man, who had not consented to their decision and action. He had himself been a disciple of Jesus and was looking expectantly for the kingdom of God, but secretly, because he feared the Judean leaders.

Pilate wondered whether Jesus was already dead. Having summoned the centurion, he asked him if Jesus had died. When he learned from the centurion that it was so, Pilate gave his permission and ordered that the corpse be given to Joseph.

So Joseph, having purchased some fine linen cloth, went and removed the body. He was accompanied by Nicodemus, the man who had first visited Jesus at night. Nicodemus brought a mixture of myrrh and aloes, about forty kilos. Taking Jesus' body, the two of them wrapped it, with the spices, in strips of clean linen. This was in accordance with Judean burial customs.

At the place where Jesus was crucified, there was an orchard. Here Joseph had a new tomb, which he had had hewn out of the rock, and in which no-one had ever been laid. Because it was the Day of Preparation and since the tomb was nearby, they laid Jesus there.

Then they rolled a great stone in front of the doorway of the tomb and went away.

The Galilean women followed Joseph and sat, watching, opposite the tomb. They noted where Jesus' body was laid. Then they returned home and prepared ointments, perfumes and spices. But they rested on the Sabbaths in obedience to the commandment.

And the Sabbaths were about to begin…

CHAPTER 26

Friday & Saturday

Friday – 15th Nisan
Special Sabbath

The following day, the one after Preparation Day, the chief priests and the Pharisees got together and went to Pilate and said, "Sir, we remember that while he was still alive that deceiving impostor said, 'After three days I will be raised.' Therefore command that the grave be guarded until after the third day in case his disciples come and steal the body. Then they will say to the people that he has been raised from the dead. So the last deception will be worse than the first."

"You have a guard," Pilate responded. "Now go and make it as secure as you know how."

So they went and made the grave secure by putting a seal *(of authority)* on the stone and posting the guard.

Saturday – 16th Nisan
A normal Sabbath day

PART 4

The New Age
The Kingdom Inaugurated

I've used the term 'New Age' because in a very real way a new age started with the resurrection of Jesus - more so than with his birth. Through his death on the cross and triumph over sin and death by the resurrection, Jesus made it possible for people to have a relationship with God without the need for a human intermediary or any prescribed ritual. Through his death, the one born to be king of Israel and indeed king over all the earth, enabled his kingdom to be established as one completely unlike any other earthly kingdom. His ascension marked his enthronement by which he opened the way for the Holy Spirit to come and multiply his work on earth, making the power of the Spirit available to all believers. It was truly the beginning of a new age in which believers are called to make more disciples who will impact every aspect of society around the world with the message and practice of the kingdom of God.

The other books of the New Testament indicate that this new age of the Holy Spirit will continue until Jesus appears as King of Kings. It is only a foretaste of the 'age to come' when there will be an unimaginable renewed heaven and earth for believers to enjoy in their own resurrected bodies.
Science-fiction and human reasoning have no concept of what this amazing future will be like.

CHAPTER 27

Death Invader

Sunday, 17th Nisan[32]
Feast of Firstfruits[33]
Guards floored

Very early in the morning, on the first day of the week, while it was still dark, a sizeable earthquake occurred. Having come from heaven, an angel of the Lord approached the tomb, flicked aside the stone then sat on top of it. His appearance was like lightning; his clothing was as white as snow. Shaken with fear of him, the guards had become like dead men.

Shock for spice girls

The Sabbath was over, so as dawn was breaking, Mary of Magdala, Mary the mother of James, Joanna, and Salome went to the tomb taking the spices they had bought and prepared, so that they might anoint Jesus' body. Other women were with them too.

On the way they had kept asking each other, "Who will roll the stone out of the doorway of the tomb for us?"

But, arriving as the sun rose, as they looked up, they clearly saw that the stone, which was massive, had been rolled away.

Having entered the tomb, they did not find the body of the Lord

Jesus. While they were at a loss wondering about this, suddenly two men in dazzling clothes were beside them.

Utterly amazed and terrified, the women bowed their faces to the ground.

One, like a young man, sat on the right side. He said to them, "Don't be alarmed, I know that you're looking for Jesus the Nazarene, the one who was crucified. Why do you look for the living one among the dead? He's not here; He has risen! Come and see the place where they laid him. Then go quickly and tell his disciples, including Peter, 'He has risen from the dead and is going ahead of you into Galilee. There you will see him. Remember how he told you while you were in Galilee, 'It is necessary for the Son of Man to be delivered into the hands of sinful men and be crucified and on the third day to be raised again." Then they remembered his words.

Seized with fear yet filled with joy, the women fled, trembling from the tomb, to report these matters to the disciples.

They said nothing to anyone on the way, because they were so afraid.

Spin doctors

While the women were on their way, some of the guards went into the city and reported to the chief priests everything that had happened. The chief priests met with the elders and resolved to bribe the soldiers with sufficient silver, instructing them to say, 'His disciples came during the night while we were sleeping and stole him away.' They said, "If this report comes to the governor's attention, we shall reassure him and keep you out of trouble."

So the soldiers took the money and did as they had been instructed. (This story has been widely circulated among the Judeans to this very day.)

Disciples in a spin

When the women returned from the tomb, they told everything to the eleven apostles and all the others who were mourning and weeping with them.

When they heard that Jesus was alive they refused to believe, because the women's words seemed like nonsense to them.

Peter, however, and the other disciple (the one Jesus loved), set out for the tomb. Both were running together, but the other disciple ran faster than Peter and came to the tomb first. He stooped down and peering in he saw the strips of linen lying there but he did not go in. Simon Peter came following him, he entered the tomb. He saw the linen cloths lying there, as well as the face cloth that had been around Jesus' head. This cloth was folded up by itself and placed apart from the linen. The other disciple, who had arrived at the tomb first, also went inside. He saw and believed. (But they still did not understand from Scripture that Jesus *had* to rise from the dead.)

The disciples went back to their homes perplexed, wondering what had happened.

Mary's close encounter

But Mary (of Magdala) stood outside the tomb weeping. As she wept, she stooped to look into the tomb and saw the two angels in white, seated where Jesus' body had been lying, one at the head and the other at the foot.

They asked her, "Woman, why are you weeping?"

"Because they have taken my Lord away," she said, "and I don't know where they've placed him." Having said this, she turned around and saw Jesus standing there, but she did not realise that it was Jesus.

"Greetings, dear woman," he said, "why are you weeping? Whom are you seeking?"

Supposing that he was the gardener, she said, "Sir, if you've carried him away, tell me where you've placed him, and I'll take him away."

Jesus said to her, "Mary."

She turned towards him and cried out in Aramaic, "Rabboni!" (which means Teacher).

She clasped his feet and worshipped him.

Jesus said, "Don't cling on to me, because I haven't yet ascended to the Father. But go to my brothers and tell them, 'I am ascending to my Father and your Father, to my God and to your God.'"

Mary went to the disciples announcing the news: "I've seen the Lord!" Then she told them the things he had said to her.

Another stunning encounter

That very day, two of the disciples were travelling to a village called Emmaus, some seven to eight miles distant from Jerusalem. Their conversation concerned everything that had happened. While they were talking and discussing these things, Jesus himself came near and began walking along with them. However, despite seeing him, somehow they were prevented from recognising him, because he seemed to have a different outward appearance.

"You're having a heated exchange as you walk along; what's it all about?" he asked.

Looking dejected, they stopped and one of them, named Cleopas, asked him, "Are you the only visitor to Jerusalem who doesn't know about the things that have happened there these past few days?"

"What things?" he asked.

"About Jesus the Nazarene," they replied, "who was a man, a prophet, dynamic in words and deeds, in the sight of God and all the people. About how both the chief priests and our rulers having handed him over to be condemned to death, crucified him. But we were hoping that he was the one who was going to liberate Israel. Now it's the third day since these things took place and to cap it all some of our womenfolk amazed us; early this morning they went to the tomb but they didn't find his body. They came back saying they'd seen a vision of angels, who said he was alive. Then some of our group went to the tomb and they too found it just as the women had said. But they didn't see him."

Then he said to them cheerily, "You chumps! How slow you are to understand and believe all that the prophets have spoken. Wasn't it necessary for the Messiah to suffer these things and then enter his glory?" So beginning with the writings of Moses, then from each of the Prophets, he interpreted to them fully all the Scriptures concerning himself.

As they approached Emmaus, it seemed as if Jesus would travel farther. But they insisted, pressing him strongly saying, "Stay with us, it's nearly evening; the day's already over." So he entered the house with them.

Then it happened that while he reclined at the table with them, having taken the bread, he gave thanks, broke it and began to give it to them. And their eyes were opened – they recognised him, but then he became invisible.

They said to one another, "Weren't our hearts on fire as he was talking with us on the road and opening up the Scriptures to us?"

That very hour they got up and returned to Jerusalem. With others who had gathered with them, they found the Eleven saying, "The Lord really has risen! He has appeared to Simon." Then the two explained what had happened on the road, and how Jesus was recognised by them by his breaking of the bread.

A third encounter

So it was that on the evening of that first day of the week, while they were still telling these things, with the doors securely shut for fear of the Judeans, suddenly Jesus came and stood amongst them and said, "Peace to you all!" They were startled and terrified, thinking they were seeing a ghost. He said to them, "Why are you frightened, and why the doubts in your hearts? Look at my hands and my feet. It's me in person! Touch me and see; because a spirit doesn't have flesh and bones, as you see I have."

Having said this, he showed them both of his hands, his feet and his side. While they were marvelling with sheer joy, yet still barely able to believe, he asked them, "Do you have anything edible here?" They gave him a piece of cooked fish and a chip off a honeycomb, which he took and ate in front of them.

Then he said to them, "While I was with you before, these are the words I spoke: 'Everything written about me in the Law of Moses, the Prophets and the Psalms must be fulfilled.'"

Then he opened their minds so they could understand the Scriptures, saying, "This is what's been written: The Messiah will suffer and will rise again from the dead on the third day. In his name repentance and the forgiveness of sins will be proclaimed to all nations, starting from Jerusalem. You are to be witnesses of these things. Look, I'm going to send you the gift which my Father has promised and then you'll be clothed with the might from on high."

Again Jesus said to them, "Peace to you! As the Father has sent me, so I'm sending you." After he said that, he breathed on them saying, "Receive the Holy Spirit. If you forgive anyone their sins, they're forgiven; if you don't forgive them, they're not forgiven."

Now Thomas, was not with them when Jesus came. So the other disciples told him, "We've seen the Lord!"

But he said to them, "Unless I see the nail marks in his hands and I put my finger into the place where the nails were, and I put my hand into his side, I will never believe."

Time for Thomas

Eight days later his disciples were inside the house again. This time Thomas was with them. Although the doors were secured, Jesus came and stood among them and said, "Peace to you!" Then he said to Thomas, "Bring your finger here and see my hands. Bring your hand and put it into my side. Don't be unbelieving but believe."

Thomas responded, "My Lord and my God!"

Then Jesus said to him, "Because you've seen me, have you believed? Blessed are those who haven't seen yet have believed."

Back to the future

After these events, at the Sea of Galilee, Jesus made himself visible to his disciples again. He showed himself like this: the eleven disciples had gone to Galilee. Simon Peter, Thomas, Nathanael from Cana in Galilee, the sons of Zebedee, and two other disciples were together. "I'm going fishing," Simon Peter said to them; they responded, "We'll come with you." So they went and boarded the boat, but during that night they caught nothing.

Just after daybreak, Jesus stood on the shore; however the disciples did not realise that it was him.

He called out to them, "Fellows, you don't have any fish, do you?" "No," they answered.

He then said, "Cast the net to the right side of the boat and you'll find some." They threw the net out but they were not strong enough to haul it in because of the huge quantity of fish.

Then that disciple whom Jesus loved said to Peter, "It's the Lord!" As soon as Simon Peter heard him say that, he wrapped his outer garment around himself (because he was unclothed) and plunged into the sea. But the other disciples came in the boat, dragging the net of fish, as they were not far from land – about a hundred metres. When they had gone ashore, they saw a charcoal fire there, with fish lying on it, and some bread.

Jesus said to them, "Bring some of the fish you've just caught."

So Simon Peter went and hauled the net onto the land. It was full of large fish, a hundred and fifty three *varieties*, but even with so many the net did not split. Jesus said to them, "Come and eat some breakfast." Now not one of the disciples was daring enough to ask him, "Who are you?" They knew it was the Lord. Jesus then came, took the bread and gave it to them, and likewise the fish. (This was now the third time, after he was raised from the dead, that Jesus had shown himself to these disciples.)

When they had eaten, Jesus said to Simon Peter, "Simon, son of John, do you LOVE me more than these?"

"Yes, Lord," he said, "you know that I love of you."

Jesus said, "Feed my lambs."

Again, a second time, Jesus said, "Simon, son of John, do you LOVE me?"

He answered, "Yes, Lord, you know that I love you."

Jesus said, "Shepherd my sheep."

The third time he said to him, "Simon, son of John, do you love me?"

Peter was grieved because Jesus had asked him the third time, "Do you love me?" He said, "Lord, you know all things; you know that I love you."

Jesus said, "Feed my sheep. I tell you the truth, when you were young you fastened your own belt and walked where you wanted; but when you grow old your hands will be extended and someone else will put a belt around you and carry you where you don't want to go." Jesus said this to signify the sort of death by which Peter would glorify God. Having said this, he said to him, "Follow me!"

On turning, Peter saw the disciple whom Jesus loved following them. When Peter saw him, he asked, "Lord, what about this man?"

Jesus answered, "If I want him to remain until I return, what is that to you? You follow me." Because of this, it was spread among the brothers that this disciple would not die. But Jesus did not say that he would not die; but, "If I want him to remain until I return, what is that to you?"

This is the disciple who testified to these things and who has written them down and we know that his testimony is true.

CHAPTER 28

Over to You

Promised presence and a great commission

While in Galilee, the disciples went to the mountain where Jesus had indicated they should meet. When he appeared, they worshipped him. *But some doubted*[34].

Approaching them he spoke, saying, "All authority in heaven and on the earth has been given to me. Go into all the world and proclaim the good news to the whole human race. As you go, make disciples of all people groups, baptising them in the name of the Father, the Son and the Holy Spirit. Teach them to pay attention to, and do, everything I've commanded you. The ones who believe and are baptised will be saved, but those who don't believe will be condemned. These signs will authenticate and accompany all those who believe: In my name they'll drive out demons; they'll speak in new tongues; they'll pick up snakes with their hands; if they drink any deadly poison, it won't harm them in any way; they'll lay hands on sick people who will recover. And listen! I'm with you every day, until this age is completed."

Promised power

After his suffering, Jesus showed himself alive by many infallible proofs. He appeared to his disciples during a period of forty days and spoke about the kingdom of God. Once, while eating with them, he instructed them not to leave Jerusalem, saying, "Stay in the city and wait for the gift my Father promised, which you've heard me speak about. John baptised with water, but not many days from now, you'll be baptised with the Holy Spirit."

So when they met, they kept asking him, "Lord, is this the time that you are going to restore the kingdom to Israel?" But he said to them, "It's not for you to know the times nor seasons which the Father has set by his own authority. But you will receive power when the Holy Spirit comes upon you; and you'll be my witnesses in Jerusalem, in all Judea and Samaria, and as far as the ends of the earth."

Promised happy return

Forty days after his resurrection, Jesus led out the disciples as far as Bethany, to the Mount of Olives. There he lifted his hands and blessed them. While he was blessing them, he left them, being taken up into heaven. As he was going, they looked intently up into the sky but a cloud hid him from their sight. Suddenly two men dressed in white were with them. "Men of Galilee," they said, "Why are you standing here looking into the sky? This Jesus, the one who has been taken from you into heaven, will return in the same way that you have seen him go into heaven."

They worshipped there and then returned to Jerusalem. Overflowing with joy, they stayed continually in the temple, praising God.

Later[35] the disciples went out and preached everywhere; the Lord working with them, confirming his word by accompanying miraculous signs.

★★★★★

As well as the events recorded in this book, Jesus did many other things, including miraculous signs, in the presence of his disciples. These are not recorded here because were every one of them to be written down, I suppose that even the whole world would not have room for the books that would be written.

But these events have been recorded so that you might believe that Christ the King, the Son of God, is none other than this Jesus; and that by believing you may have LIFE in his name.

GENEALOGIES

The pedigree of the Ram

> 'A recorded ram can deliver added benefits during its lifetime.'
> *English Beef and Lamb Executive*
> 'The fuller the genealogy, the more valuable the ram.'
> *Swaledale farmer, BBC 'lamb-watch' programme March 2011*

Matthew's genealogy. Matt 1:1-17 (NIV)
A record of the genealogy of Jesus Christ the son of David, the son of Abraham:

Abraham was the father of Isaac, **Isaac** the father of Jacob, **Jacob** the father of Judah and his brothers. **Judah** the father of Perez and Zerah, whose mother was Tamar.
Perez the father of Hezron, **Hezron** the father of Ram. **Ram** the father of Amminadab, **Amminadab** the father of Nahshon, **Nahshon** the father of Salmon, **Salmon** the father of Boaz, whose mother was Rahab. **Boaz** the father of Obed, whose mother was Ruth, **Obed** the father of Jesse, and **Jesse** the father of King David.
David was the father of Solomon, whose mother had been Uriah's wife. **Solomon** the father of Rehoboam, **Rehoboam** the father of Abijah, **Abijah** the father of Asa. **Asa** the father of Jehoshaphat, **Jehoshaphat** the father of Jehoram, **Jehoram** the father of Uzziah. **Uzziah** the father of Jotham, **Jotham** the father of Ahaz, **Ahaz** the father of Hezekiah. **Hezekiah** the father of Manasseh, **Manasseh** the father of Amon, **Amon** the father of Josiah, and **Josiah** the father of Jeconiah and his brothers at the time of the exile to Babylon.
After the exile to Babylon: **Jeconiah** was the father of Shealtiel, **Shealtiel** the father of Zerubbabel, **Zerubbabel** the father of Abiud.

Abiud the father of Eliakim, **Eliakim** the father of Azor, **Azor** the father of Zadok, **Zadok** the father of Akim, **Akim** the father of Eliud, **Eliud** the father of Eleazar, **Eleazar** the father of Matthan. **Matthan** the father of Jacob, and **Jacob** the father of **Joseph**, the *father*[36] of **Mary**, of whom was born Jesus, who is called Christ.

Thus there were fourteen generations in all from Abraham to David, fourteen from David to the exile to Babylon, and fourteen from the exile to the Christ.

Luke's genealogy. Luke 3:23-38 (NIV)

Joseph, the son of **Heli,** the son of **Matthat,** the son of **Levi,** the son of **Melki,** the son of **Jannai,** the son of **Joseph,** the son of **Mattathias,** the son of **Amos,** the son of **Nahum,** the son of **Esli,** the son of **Naggai,** the son of **Maath,** the son of **Mattathias,** the son of **Semein,** the son of **Josech,** the son of **Joda,** the son of **Joanan,** the son of **Rhesa,** the son of **Zerubbabel,** the son of **Shealtiel,** the son of **Neri,** the son of **Melki,** the son of **Addi,** the son of **Cosam,** the son of **Elmadam,** the son of **Er,** the son of **Joshua,** the son of **Eliezer,** the son of **Jorim,** the son of **Matthat,** the son of **Levi,** the son of **Simeon,** the son of **Judah,** the son of **Joseph,** the son of **Jonam,** the son of **Eliakim,** the son of **Melea,** the son of **Menna,** the son of **Mattatha,** the son of **Nathan,** the son of **David,** the son of **Jesse,** the son of **Obed,** the son of **Boaz,** the son of **Salmon,** the son of **Nahshon,** the son of **Amminadab,** the son of **Ram,** the son of **Hezron,** the son of **Perez,** the son of **Judah,** the son of **Jacob,** the son of **Isaac,** the son of **Abraham,** the son of **Terah,** the son of **Nahor,** the son of **Serug,** the son of **Reu,** the son of **Peleg,** the son of **Eber,** the son of **Shelah,** the son of **Cainan,** the son of **Arphaxad,** the son of **Shem,** the son of **Noah**[37], the son of **Lamech,** the son of **Methuselah,** the son of **Enoch,** the son of **Jared,** the son of **Mahalalel,** the son of **Kenan,** the son of **Enosh,** the son of **Seth,** the son of **Adam,** the son of **God.**

A Little Excursion

Four-part harmony

Before setting out on this journey I asked various people if they were aware of any gospel harmonies, but received negative replies. A trawl of bookshops produced the same result. This did surprise me since the gospels have been around for nearly 2000 years and I would have thought that this exercise would have been done already. The apparent absence of such works encouraged me to proceed. Initially I decided to use only the New International Version since it is a popular and very readable version of the Bible. However, after receiving comments on the first draft I started looking at other translations and some commentaries. I then decided to review the whole document. In the course of this undertaking I came across a harmonisation based on Moffatt's translation of the New Testament. After completing my work I was advised of a harmonisation based on the NIV and came across one based on the NIV Readers Version. I discovered also, on the internet, a translation of the Diatessaron of Tatian. This latter work, from the second century, is believed to have been one of the earliest harmonisations. For several centuries, it was in common use in the Middle East. It is believed this harmonisation was the reason that Mohammed considered there to be only one gospel.

This Translation

When the gospel writers were inspired to compile, what were

essentially summaries and eye-witness accounts of the life and times of Jesus, it is clear that they each had their own style of writing, their own emphasis and prospective readership in mind. Therefore they should, and do, read quite differently. This has made merging the stories and teachings somewhat difficult. For example, one writer may have used actual speech in a situation, while another uses reported speech. I've attempted to have a mix of both. Similarly the writers of the gospels may have used the teaching and illustrative stories (parables) of Jesus in different settings. Matthew tends to gather together sections of Jesus' teachings while Luke includes them during actual events. I have tried to use both methods but aimed to use a teaching or parable and event only once. Being the master teacher that he was, it is highly likely that, during his three years' ministry, Jesus used the same teaching and parables on a number of occasions, modifying them to suit the needs of the situation. Hence some differences in the way the gospel writers recorded some of the teachings of Jesus. I have attempted to incorporate the differences into the teachings and parables to include the different aspects.

There are very few inconsistencies in the different gospels. Each has its own unique stories or sayings. Differences can be explained by the normal discrepancies amongst eye-witnesses. When combined, they paint a fuller picture of the events described. Matthew does have a tendency to see double – two wild men amongst the tombs, two blind men at Jericho etc. He may well have been combining similar events since it is evident that the miracles and events recorded in the gospels are only a sample from an action-packed three years of ministry. I have gone along with Matthew on the odd occasion.

The majority of the original texts were written in Greek. Scholars have pointed out that the Greek of the gospels is the rough- and-ready everyday language of country folk, not some unapproachable, unreadable classical religious treatise. I've attempted to reflect this, particularly in conversations. I have sought to avoid using wooden speech e.g. 'I am', 'he will', 'he would not', 'you are' etc. and used 'I'm', he'll, he wouldn't, you're etc. which feels more natural and is particularly helpful when reading aloud; which is highly recommended. There are a number of alliterations in the Greek scripts, as well as some word play. This is not usually evident in English translations so I have attempted to include some of these, though not necessarily in the same places as in the Greek.

To illustrate modes of action and emphasis which are not readily translated by single English words, various tenses are employed by the gospel writers. Language changes over time so what a writer is believed to have wanted to say may be better expressed by a more modern word usage. This explains the numerous versions and paraphrases of the Bible available today.

The repeated challenge for Bible translators is that of deciding whether to undertake a word-for-word translation or a thought–for-thought translation. For this work I have drawn from over twenty English translations based on both of these methods. Not being a Greek scholar, I appreciate that I have stood on the shoulders of a host of skilled and competent translators. I have also taken note of interpretations of words and phrases offered by some commentators and lexicographers. Therefore there are some variations unique to this work. In some instances this has meant that the same Greek words have been translated differently on different occasions in order to expand their meaning. In other instances one English word is used to translate more than one Greek word, but the directly translated English word does not bring out the different meanings intended. I have tackled this in the case of the two English words 'life' and 'love' by using different word formats. Each of these words can be translated from three different Greek words – only two of which in the case of 'love' are used in the gospels:-

Life: Gk. Zoe – chiefly meaning life as God has it, life in its fullness, from which, as a consequence of their rebellion against God, a person is alienated.

This has been expressed in the text as 'LIFE'.

Gk. Bios – meaning one's life on earth, or the means by which it is sustained.
Gk. Psuche – the person or personality, the inner life of a person.
Both are expressed in the text as 'life'.

Love: Gk. Agape – expressing the highest kind of self-giving love which expects nothing in return.

Is the essential nature of God. It is a result of a decision of the will. Almost exclusively a characteristic of Christianity. Expressed in the text as 'LOVE'.

Gk. Phileo – the love of natural inclination, affection. Expressed in the text as 'love'.

Traditions

During his ministry, Jesus was constantly at odds with the religious leaders of his day. This was because he was seeking to bring ordinary men and women into a relationship with his father but was hindered by the rites and traditions which had grown up in Judaism.

Traditions, religious or otherwise, usually arise out of an experience of life, but then develop a life of their own. Often the original reason for the tradition or practice is lost so they end up as a dead ritual.

By the time Jesus came on the scene Judaism was cluttered with hundreds of rules and regulations. This led to people going through religious motions but never really connecting with the living God. Sadly the same can be said of Christianity. Over the centuries numerous rites and traditions have sprung up in every expression of the Christian faith. Some may be helpful, but they are pointless if they separate people from the very God they were supposed to point to. It is amazing that rites and traditions are often elevated above what the Bible says. It may come as a surprise to some that in fact, in biblical Christianity, there are no special holy places, holy people or holy days. Worship can take place anywhere at any time. All believers are called 'saints'; the events of the life of Jesus and the early church can be celebrated at any time or not at all – although there are biological and social reasons to take rest, change routine and celebrate.

So, the fact that in this text the day of the crucifixion has been identified as a Thursday rather than the usual 'Good Friday' is of little consequence. The important point is that Jesus was crucified and rose from the dead. Two consecutive Sabbath days occurring during the 'last week' would not require any special mention by the gospel writers as it was not so unusual at feast times. However, John's gospel does mention 'special' in relation to the Sabbath in the last week. This may suggest that an extra Sabbath day was meant. For me, a Thursday death fits in more accurately with Jesus' statements that he would rise on the third day and be in the grave three nights. Again the point is one of interest rather than contention.

Bibliography

In compiling this work I have drawn ideas, words and phrases from the following:

Bible versions and translations:
Authorised Version (King James)
New King James Version, Thomas Nelson Inc. 1982.
New International Version, Zondervan, 1994.
New Living Translation, Tyndale House Publishers Inc, 1996, 2004.
New American Standard Version, Lockman Foundation, 1977.
New Revised Standard Version, National Council of the Churches of Christ, U.S.A.,1990.
Contemporary English Version, Collins, 2000.
English Standard Version, Collins, 2007.
The Message, *Eugene Peterson*, NavPress, 2003.
Cover to Cover Complete (incorporates Holman Christian Standard Bible), CWR, 2007.
New Testament, Good News Bible, Collins, 2005 edition.
The New Greek-English Interlinear New Testament, Tyndale House Publishers Inc.,1990.
The New Testament, A New Translation, *J Moffatt*, Hodder & Stoughton, 1934.

The New Testament in Modern Speech, *R.F. Weymouth*, Hodder & Stoughton, 1938.

The New Testament, *Nicholas King*, Kevin Meyhew, 2004.

New Testament, *J G Anderson*, Anderson Prison Ministries, 1984

The Gospels in Modern English, *J.B. Phillips*, Fontana, 1958.

The Four Gospels and The Revelation, *Richard Lattimore*, Dorset Press, N.Y., 1979.

The Four Gospels, *E.V. Rieu*, The Penguin Classics, Penguin Books, 1952.

The Four Gospels, *Norman Marrow*, White Crescent Press, 1977.

Other:

Expository Dictionary of New Testament Words, *W.E. Vine*, Oliphants, 22nd imp. 1979

Matthew, An introduction & commentary, Tyndale N.T. Commentaries, *R.V.G. Tasker*, IVP, 1978

The Gospel According to St Mark, **an introduction and commentary**, Tyndale N.T. Commentaries, *R.A. Cole*, Tyndale Press, 1966.

Mark in the Gk New Testament, Wuest's Word Studies, *K S Wuest*, Pickering & Inglis, 1950

Commentary on The Gospel of Luke, New London Commentaries on the N.T., *N Gledenhuys*, Marshall Morgan & Scott, 3rd Ed.,1956.

Luke, Tyndale N.T. Commentaries, *Leon Morris*, IVP, Revised Edition, 1989.

John, Tyndale N.T. Commentaries, *R.V.G. Tasker*, IVP, 1988.

John: The Gospel of Belief, New London Commentaries on the N.T. ,*M.C. Tenny*, Marshall, Morgan & Scott, 2nd Ed, 1954

The Four Gospels, The Armoury Commentary, Ed. General F Coutts, Hodder, 1973

A Bible Commentary for English Readers, Vol VI, The Four Gospels, Ed. C J Ellicott, Cassell & Co. 1888?

Other gospel harmonisations:
The Life of Jesus – more than a prophet, *David Holdaway*, Soverign World, 2006.
A harmonisation based on the New International Version of the Bible. The genealogies are excluded. This book has additional chapters on the historicity and uniqueness of Jesus and the authority of the New Testament.

The Four Gospels as One, *Wendy M Hearn*, Egon Publishers Ltd, 1996.
A harmonisation based mainly on Moffatt's translation, the Authorised Version, Good News Bible and the New English Bible. This work has supplementary material on the Jewish feasts and the temple.

All About Jesus, *Roger Quy*, Authentic Publishing, 2007.
A harmonisation based on the New International Readers Version. This has some American idioms. The graphic overprint at the beginning of each chapter makes reading difficult. Additional notes are included to explain references to events or people mentioned in other books of the Bible.

Becoming a Life Receiving Believer

Being a believer is more than just giving a mental agreement to the truths in the gospels. It is also more than trying to live life following the teachings of Jesus. Many who do these things call themselves 'Christians'. Others think that because they have been born in a certain race or country they are automatically Christians. The gospels show that this is not the case.

No-one is born a Christian. The term 'Christian' is not in the gospels. It only appears a few times in the New Testament: used by non-believers to describe those who were living like Jesus.

(Perhaps to avoid confusion it would be better if that were the case today and people just called themselves 'believers' or disciples/followers of Jesus and let others call them 'Christian' if their believing and consequent lifestyle reflects the teachings of Jesus!)

Having read the gospel story, you will have seen that the good news that is being proclaimed is that Jesus has come i) to fulfil the hopes and expectations of the peoples of Israel, ii) to widen the scope, of who is to be considered as being the people of God, to all nations, iii) to inaugurate the Kingdom of God on earth and iv) to demonstrate God's passion for people, and opening the way for everyone to have the opportunity of a personal relationship with God for themselves.

This personal relationship is what God wants for you. He has taken the initiative. However that relationship is impossible when our selfish human nature rebels against the rule of God. We want to live life how we please and to come to God on our terms, if at all.

Jesus clearly declares that he is the only way to God and the way back into a relationship with Him is available for us by repentance. This is the narrow way Jesus speaks about. Repentance means turning from going in one direction (ours) to going in another (God's).

We need to recognise and agree that all of our 'going our own way' is sin and rebellion. It is at odds with his kingdom. We need to acknowledge that Jesus is who he claimed to be – God who has come in the flesh – and that he took the penalty for all our sins upon himself on the cross, and there is nothing else we can do to make amends. That's the good news – we haven't got to do anything since Jesus has already done it all – apart from repenting and asking for his forgiveness, receiving his offer of salvation and asking him to take control of our lives.

All this can be vocalised in a simple prayer. You can do it anywhere at any time.

It's best then to tell someone what you have done. It will help to seal it in your own life.

You have then been 'born from above' into the family of God (the church). You can then start building that important life-fulfilling relationship, which will last through all eternity, and discover how your life can be used to extend the kingdom of God in the world today.

To help you grow in your relationship with God and discover his plan for you, it's best if you can find a group of other believers who can help you take those essential first steps of being baptised in water, praying, and being filled with the Holy Spirit.

For some initial help check out the local churches that may be running the Alpha Course www.uk.alpha.org/findacourse – or contact: info@bridgestreetchurch.org and we'll do our best to help you.

Notes

1   *'The Supreme Being'*, 'The Ground of all Being', 'The Word' or 'Logos' were all terms used in the Greek philosophy of the day to denote the controlling reason behind the universe; the all-pervasive Mind which ruled and gave meaning to all things. It was one of the purest and general concepts of that ultimate intelligence that is called God. John in his gospel uses the vocabulary of that time. However he redefines the term, not as a philosophical concept, but in the light of a particular person – about whom he goes on to write about.

2   *Christ* is the Greek word used to translate the Hebrew **'Messiah'**. Both mean **'Anointed One'**. In the Old Testament kings, prophets and priests were anointed. The Old Testament writings indicated that at some time in history, God's superhero would appear. Among other things, he would be a mighty king from the line of the great king David.

    During the Roman occupation there was an expectation that the Messiah would come, free the nation from the tyranny of Rome and restore national pride and prosperity.

3   *Mary* – the Greek version of the Hebrew name 'Miriam'. *Jesus* – the Greek version of the Hebrew name 'Joshua'.

    The more familiar names have been used throughout.

4   *Lamb* – The lamb was a common sacrificial animal, particularly at the special feast times e.g. at Passover, when a lamb would be eaten to remember the time when the blood of a lamb was put on the door posts, which effectively brought the Israelites deliverance from slavery in Egypt.

    But this was no baby animal; for Passover in particular it was to be a year old male – so more correctly it was a young **ram.**

    It was a ram that was caught in the thicket on Mt Moriah when Abraham was about to slay his son Isaac – at the spot where the temple was later built. As will be seen later, John the Baptist refers to Jesus as the Lamb of God.

5   *Magians* – Not to be confused with magicians. The identity and number of those who brought gifts to the baby Jesus is unknown. A possibility used here is that they were priests from Mesopotamia or experts in Persian religion from the Median tribe.

6   There is possibly a play on the Hebrew letters for Nazareth and Branch 'n-z-r' and fulfils the prophecies of Isaiah 11:1 and Jeremiah 23:5, 33:15. There is no O.T. prophecy about Jesus being a Nazarene or taking the vow of a Nazarite.

7   *Pharisees* - The Pharisees were a religious and political group who tended to be aloof from the rest of the populace. They practised a strict form of religious observance, attempting to apply every detail of the Law. In doing so they had invented many traditions and insisted they be observed by everyone. These became a burden of trifling political correctness.

8   *Sadducees* – The Sadducees saw themselves as followers of Zadoc, the high priest in King David's day. They came from powerful and rich families, being highly influential, particularly with respect to temple worship. They did not believe in a resurrection nor an afterlife.

9   *Lake of Gennesaret* is interchangeable with Lake/*Sea of Galilee* and Sea/Lake Tiberias.

10   The great *ruling council* in Jerusalem – **The Sanhedrin** – consisting of 71 members including scribes, elders and prominent members of the high priestly families some whom would be Pharisees. The High Priest presided. The Council had powers to deal with many cases, particularly those relating to the interpretation of the Law. They had power to pass sentence of death, but this had to be ratified by the Roman procurator.

11   *Everlasting life & eternal life*: these terms refer to the type and quality of life to be experienced by believers. For the 'Christian' it starts at the moment of belief and repentance and goes on past the cessation of natural human life. It was also a hope associated with Judaism.

12   *Sabbath* – the day of rest and worship – 7th day of the week. There were strict regulations about what could be done or not done on the Sabbath, far exceeding anything in the Old Testament law.

13   *Synagogue* – A local meeting place for worship and teaching.

14   *Gentiles* – a word referring to all the other nations who were considered not to be part of the chosen people of Israel and followers of Judaism.

15   *Tax collectors* – These were considered to be the lowest form of life since they were working for the Romans and probably accumulating wealth for themselves at the expense of the ordinary people.

16   'The Way' was the term given for the means of access to God through the temple – from the outer court to the Holy of Holies – the latter was accessed only once each year by the High Priest. The name was given also to the Christian life as practised by the early believers. They were known as 'Followers of the Way'. The first Christians didn't call themselves Christians

but it was a name given to them by unbelievers who observed their life and declared that they were living a Christ-like life.

17   Traditionally guests would not sit but recline at a low table. They would lie on low couches, resting on their left elbow, eating with their right hand. Their feet would be stretched out behind. During the meal the sandals were taken off.

18   *Beelzebub* – Chief of demons, Satan – could mean Lord of the Flies, or Dung Lord – a name used of a Philistine god.

19   *Gadarenes* is interchangeable with, Gerasenes – region to south east of the Sea of Galilee.

20   *Magadan* – also known as Magdala and Dalmanutha

21   *The Feast of Tabernacles* – The last of the three great annual feasts that men in `particular were expected to attend. It was a joyful 8-day celebration of the fruit harvest about October time. A feature of the feast was that people were expected to live in leafy shelters as reminder of the 40 years in the wilderness. Even the sacrificial lambs were covered with palm branches. Towards the end of the celebrations there was a water-pouring ceremony.

22   *The Feast of Dedication* (or Lights – Hanukkah) was celebrated about 25th December. It commemorated the rededication of the temple by the Maccabees after the emperor Antiochus Epiphanes had used the altar to make sacrifices to heathen gods.

23   *Examining the Lamb*: to ensure they were free from faults, it was the custom to examine the lambs which were to be sacrificed at Passover. The lamb was identified and selected on 10th Nisan ready for slaughter on 14th Nisan. Unwittingly the Pharisees, Sadducees, lawyers and chief priests were examining the Passover lamb to end all Passovers lambs. They all attempted to find fault with Jesus from 10th right through to the trials on the 14th – but failed – he was declared faultless.

24   Passover effectively became part of the *Feast of Unleavened Bread*. The regulations say that the Passover lamb should be killed on the 14th of the month and eaten at twilight, towards 6 p.m. i.e. starting late on the 14th and probably finishing on the 15th. The 15th is the proper start of the Feast of Unleavened Bread, although Passover day and the week from the 15th are often referred to as the Feast of Passover or the Feast of Unleavened Bread.
'Preparation Day' could mean the day before Passover day, Passover day itself in preparation for Unleavened Bread or even the day before a normal Sabbath. It should be noted that the first day (and last) of the Feast of Unleavened Bread was an additional Sabbath. Therefore, depending on how the feast fell, it was possible to have two Sabbath days in the same week. They could be

consecutive days, i.e. a special Sabbath for the feast and the usual 'Saturday' Sabbath. (A likely possibility for this particular week.)

Old Testament references: Exodus 12, Leviticus 23, Numbers 28, Deuteronomy 16.

25 The *Passover Feast* day would begin at this time but traditionally the Passover meal itself would be eaten at the end of the 14th – almost 24 hours later. Jesus was sitting down to the supper at the earliest possible time on the 14th.

26 During the ritual Passover meal a piece of unleavened bread would be taken and broken – part would be hidden and later found. It was known as the 'bread of affliction'. It represented the coming of the, as yet unseen, Messiah. It is possible that this is *The Bread* that Jesus took. This act would be packed with significance for those present. Similarly, to symbolise the expected coming of the messianic age, at the end of the meal a fourth drink of wine would be taken. A fifth goblet of wine was known as Elijah's cup and possibly would not be used, thus symbolising the yet to come Messiah. This could be *The Cup* that Jesus took – again demonstrating to those present that he was the Messiah – and therefore the dawn of a new messianic era had arrived.

27 There were two *cock-crowings*, the first straight after mid-night (3rd watch of the night) and the second immediately before dawn (4th watch).

28 A *'band of soldiers'* (King James' Version and others) also translated as Cohort. A cohort had 600 men. 'A band' may have been referring to a 'manipuli,' believed to be the equivalent of a third of a cohort. So here we may be looking at a **detachment of some 200 soldiers**!

29 *Praetorium* – Military headquarters and home of the Roman governor/procurator/prefect – Pilate

30 Brutal *flogging* was usual before any crucifixion. The whip would be a lash of two or three strips of leather to which pieces of bone or metal were attached. The lashes would cut the skin while the bone and metal would create deep contusions. It is likely that two people would be engaged in the flogging while the victim was tied naked to a pole with their hands above their head. There was no limit to a Roman flogging and it is likely that over a hundred lashes would be inflicted to the back, buttocks and lower limbs causing massive haemorrhaging and weakness or even death of the victim. It was usual not to weaken the victim to the extent that they would not be able to carry their cross

31 The curtain, or *veil*, (the parokhet), was the richly embroidered linen material separating the Holy Place from the Holy of Holies in the tabernacles and then in the temple. The Holy of Holies was the place representing and exhibiting the presence of God. Access was by way of the veil but was limited to the High Priest on one day only in the year. The tearing of the veil was in effect God

saying that the way into his presence was now open for everyone. A line from the hymn 'To God be the glory' by Fanny J Crosby, effectively sums up what happened when Jesus died:

"*… who yielded his life, an atonement for sin and opened the life-gate that all may go in*".

32   Interestingly the 17th day of the first month in the Hebraic religious calendar (the seventh month of the civic calendar) is associated with new beginnings – Noah's ark rested on Ararat on this date and the crossing of the Red Sea took place on this date.

It seems that some divine time manager was at work to ensure that in this particular year the 17th Nisan fell on the first day of the new week!

33   The *Feast of Firstfruits* was a third element of the celebration week which included Passover and Unleavened Bread. This feast was celebrated on the first day of the week following the normal Sabbath after Passover. It was a thanksgiving for the fruits of the land the people of Israel enjoyed after their 40 years wanderings in the wilderness. Also it was a thanksgiving for the first token of the year's crops – the barley harvest – in anticipation of more crops and fruits to be harvested later in the year.

34   The apostle Paul writes that Jesus appeared to over 500 people at one time. This appearance in Galilee may have been that occasion. It would account for the statement that '*some doubted*'. (see 1 Corinthians 15:6.)

35   **Later** - After they had been baptised with the Holy Spirit - but you'll have to read the book of Acts to find out more…

36   NIV and most other versions say 'husband' of Mary – but this could be Mary's genealogy. The word translated 'husband' means 'man' in any role, so could equally be father or husband. If it is husband there is a generation short in the list and we have two different genealogies for Joseph. It is quite possible that Mary's father, like her husband, was called Joseph.

37   As a matter of interest it's been pointed out that an interpretation of the names of the first ten patriarchs listed in the Torah/Old Testament can provide a summary of the good news of Jesus – the God who became mortal and by who's death mankind is brought into the rest of a right relationship with God.